So Prays My Soul

Spirited Prayers from a Heart Transformed

By Deanna Nickel Rose

Xulon
PRESS

Contents

Introduction

*P*rayer has been an integral part of my life for as long as I can
remember. There is power in prayer to make both gradual
and drastic life changes. The major changes are to the person praying.
As prayer becomes more comfortable during our daily activities, the
more truthful and intimate our relationship with God and all of God's
creation becomes. We then begin to more fully understand that it
is better to be connected to God than to be correct in our theology.
I think we can relate to God in many ways as prayer can be in a
myriad of forms. A brief appreciation for the beauty of a tree or the
vastness of an ocean is a prayer. Prayers can be repeated by rote as
in the Lord's Prayer or the Rosary; they can be a child God blessing
family and friends at bedtime or prayer can be a musical uplifting.
Contemplative prayer in a variety of meditation styles can especially
open the mind and soul to be more receptive to the 'knowing' of the
Holy Spirit. It is when we are alone with God that God becomes more
real. In this life, we won't have all the answers, nevertheless, God's
love and grace shines within our being. We can argue, express anger
and ask difficult questions. God is a big boy and can take it. I think
God appreciates our honesty and our gut feelings. God knows that
sometimes we just need to vent. At the other end of the spectrum,
sharing smiley moments or laughter with God can be special. We can
pray to God with our eyes wide open while focusing on a cross or
nature. Hands can be folded or open in a gesture of welcoming the
spirit of God. In short, just relax and let the communication happen.

Communication is dualistic. Sometimes we are so busy doing the praying that we don't stop to listen in mental silence for God's feedback. Psalm 46:10 is the first prayer in this book that asks us to be still and know. Prayer beads are a good way to experience a two way communication. I have included instructions for making and using prayer beads.

Some of the prayers in this book are adapted from prayers I wrote for worship services so they may be used for personal prayer or as a guide for worship gatherings. Some of the prayers or issues in this book of prayers may seem repetitive. There are basic issues that we need to ponder on a regular basis such as God's love, peace, forgiveness and our purpose in this life. According to Martin Luther, the Lord's Prayer includes seven petitions. I think most prayers should include an expression of appreciation for God's awesomeness and gratitude for His gifts of love, grace and so much more. The more you connect and communicate with God the more natural it will become. It takes practice to learn almost everything in life. God knows you better than you know yourself. God understands you better than anyone else. God loves you all the time just as you are. So do not be afraid to be yourself without any pretensions when talking with God. If this book helps you in any way to become closer to God, then I am thankful. The cover of this book is a message of transformation. The cross transforms us through the sacrifice of Christ and the grace of God to an eternally graceful being filled with the greatest power in the universe- the power of love. We are like the caterpillar which is wonderfully cool, however, when prayerfully connecting with God we transform into an even more beautiful and purposeful person. The butterfly pollinates flowers. We will pollinate people to bloom with the knowledge of God's love.

You will notice when the word, 'You' refers to God in this book, it is capitalized. Don't you think God deserves a capital Y?

Dedication

I humbly dedicate, *So Prays My Soul,* to God who taught me how to live well and inspired me to love more fully. God has been with me and accepted me with all my hang ups and quirks. I am thankful that God has shared my roller coaster ride of joys and sorrows along the way of living and that someday God will guide my transformation into the next. I also dedicate this book to my grandchildren.

Thanks a Bunch

*P*eople say that it takes a village to raise a child. Well, I found out that it also takes a village to write and publish a book. *So Prays My Soul* would not be in your hands without the help and encouragement of my family, friends, church friends and especially the inspiration and gentle nudging of the Holy Spirit to continue on. I am gratefully blessed to be the daughter of Earl and Dorothy (Hetrick) Nickel who passed on family traditions of faith in a loving God and positive values. I am so thankful for my grandparents, aunts and uncles who nurtured each child in the family tree with patience and humor as they taught me, my brothers and cousins life lessons The legacy of our lives continues for a multitude of generations. Thanks to my cousin, Milton Hetrick, Jr. and Frieda (Hetrick) Ried who traced our family's rich history of faith while settling in America. Their legacy of living the good faith in action continues. 'Settling' seems like such a comfy word. Settling was actually so much more. Settling in Oak Harbor, Ohio was clearing swampy wet land without modern vehicles and tools. Settling was surviving long days of hard work and driving to church on dirt roads in horse drawn buggies or later in cars with no heat. The grocery store was the family garden, the chicken coop, the orchard, the woods for game, the creek for fish and the barn for milk. They still had time to help neighbors, care for the elderly in their own homes and share meals cooked on a wood burning stove. Some of my ancestors fought in the Revolution, joined the Union army in the Civil War and served during WWII. We are influenced by our ancestors whom we have not met and sometimes by people who share only a few moments in time with us. Without their influence, my life and the prayers of my soul would not be what they are. May your legacy of a prayer filled faith continue on and on and on to be a blessing.

A major influence to my prayer life has been my lifelong connection of learning, worshiping, participating and praying in a church. A church or denomination is a way to be introduced to and getting to know God more fully and clearly. Church affiliation has been crucial in nurturing my faith and my prayer life. When experiencing negative situations or people (Over a lifetime there can be many) I try to remember that the church is not a rest home for saints. It is a hospital for sinners. The positives of gathering with people of faith and the opportunity to serve God in religious sponsored programs serving people in need far outweigh the negatives.

A special smiley face of thanks to Sue Iceman and Jan Saunders who edited my prayers. Even with spell-check, it was not an easy breezy task. Sharing creative ideas, faith and family history with my Sista, Jan have been priceless. Thanks also to Trudy Woods who helped this techno challenged author compile all the prayers etc, into one document for submission and helped me tackle the frustrating computer glitches.

Testimonials for Deanna Rose

She served on the Church Council, Social Ministry, as well as the Worship and Music Committee. Deanna was especially supportive in her role as a member of my Mutual Ministry/Staff Support committee. She is an excellent caregiver to the homebound members as a Pastoral Partner Deanna has excellent communication skills and brings out her warm spiritual side whenever she is in a worship setting. She is a delight when delivering children's sermons and does it with enthusiasm. She is wonderfully creative with her crafting of words and prayers. She lives out her faith in the way she serves Jesus, her Savior. I, personally, appreciate that Deanna's deep spiritual life comes through in her ability to put into words the daily struggles and individual's needs to connect with their God. She has a special way of comforting and supporting people in all stages of life.

Deaconess Jeanette Rebeck, Pastoral Associate

So my Mom, Deanna Rose, wrote this book that you're holding in your hands right now. I just think that is really cool! I am picturing you nestled in some nook and cranny in your house with a hot cup of coffee and warm fireplace as you read and absorb my Mom's book. That thought gives me so much joy and peace as I think abouit. I am so proud of my Mom for her vision and fortitude to write this book and I am grateful for the love and energy she put into it all for the glory of God. She is a very special lady and has been a blessing, whether I realized it or not, in my life. I pray that this book gives you insight and encouragement to know, love and serve our Lord today, tomorrow and for days and years to come. I hope that this book will infuse the gifts of the spirit into your life and that when you finish this book and either put it on a shelf or pass it to a good friend that you have more…joy, peace, patience, kindness, goodness, generosity, charity, gentleness, faithfulness, self-control and modesty.

God bless you and your family, Joel Woods

PRAYERS OF REFLECTION

Be Still and Know That I Am God
Psalm 46:10 RSV

Take a slow deep breath through your nose and then exhale slowly through your mouth. Relax your body and open your mind as you let the words of Psalm 46 seep into your body, mind and soul. Pause between each phrase.

Be still and know that I am God.

Be still and know that I am.

Be still and know.

Be still.

Be.

To be a Follower, I Must Listen
John 10:27

Lord, I pray and pray and pray. Sometimes I pray with awe and sometimes with gratitude. There are times when I am overwhelmed and pray for help. I want to follow in Your way of living but I'm not always sure which road to take. As I wend my way every day I wonder if I miss opportunities to grow in faith and feel the oneness of our relationship. Since prayer is a two way relationship I need to stop and listen. Lord, I am open to following You. *Relax as you sit comfortably and then place your hands palm up on your thighs. Take a deep breath or two and slowly empty your mind as you concentrate on your breathing. Relax Smile Listen*

Love You Lord

May My Salvation be Revealed
I Peter 1:4-5

Oh God of wonder, God of light, thank You for being in my life. May today be all I need it to be. May the peace of God and the freshness of the Holy Spirit rest in my thoughts, rule in my dreams and conquer all my fears. God, may You manifest Yourself in ways I have never experienced. May my joys be sustained, my dreams closer to being fulfilled and my prayers answered according to Your will. I pray that my faith in a loving God reaches a new height. I pray my successes be increased. I pray for peace, healing, health, happiness, prosperity, joy, truth and an undying love for You, Lord. I reflect on the following prayer thoughts as I make them personal to me:

God of love, thank You for
Lord, help me to deal thoughtfully with
Holy Spirit inspire my journey of faith
Holy Spirit give moments of clarity to guide those to whom You are unknown
Lord, help me to reach outside of my comfort zone so that I
I pray that my family and I will prosper
I will share my prosperity by
Even though I still miss them, I am glad my loved ones are with You in a place beautiful beyond my comprehension.
God, thank You for all the blessings in my life. Amen

Seeds of Faith

Matthew 13:1-9 18-23
Selah means to stop and think so after Selah in this prayer, pause, so you can think about what you just prayed to God.

God of all things tangible and intangible. You created the soil of the earth and the soil of my soul. Both can be fertile ground for wonderful things to grow and bloom. Every flower planted adds beauty to the universe. Vegetables gardened add sustenance for our bodies.

The abundant richness of the earth is a gift that we need to treasure and take care of. **Selah**

The soil of my soul also needs to be nurtured so that I can bloom and be fruitful in my actions. I want my faith to be grounded like the oak tree that just keeps growing- both into the earth's foundation for stability and also above ground as it branches toward the sky. I pray that while my feet are planted on solid fertile ground, the eyes of my soul reach toward Your light so that I might perceive Your truth and Your will for me. **Selah**

I am thankful for those who listen to the Holy Spirit and plant seeds of faith and love in all corners and niches of the earth.

Thank You for my family and friends who help to water my faith. **Selah**

Lord, You did good when You created the animals of the earth. We can learn so much from them. I am thankful for my own pets. **Selah**

In the name of Jesus, I pray Your will be done in all things and that I live in Your will. Amen

Chatting on My Porch
I John 4: 7-14

Lord, if I could sit on the porch with You on a sunny day, I wonder what we would talk about. What questions would I ask You? Would we even need to talk? I think we would smile a lot. I would feel so loved seeing acceptance of me in Your eyes, Lord. Acceptance just as I am. I can almost hear You saying, "I'm not through with you yet because You have more stuff to do in My name. If I were sitting on the porch with You, Jesus, I would know when You left, that I would see You again.

Hmm. Actually, I can sit with You any day on my porch, patio or anywhere and chat with you.

Lord, I hope I do not take Your goodness and grace for granted. In Jesus' name, Your will be done in the Universe. Amen

Reflections on a Good Life With Dark Days
Matthew 11:28-29

I reflect on God the Father, God the Creator... God of heaven and earth- Creator of Life— — You are so great, so awesome. I am so blessed to know You and even more blessed to be called Your child. Wow! A child of such a loving God.

Lord, I reflect on the good things in my life and how I can make life more meaningful to myself and to others. Thank you, Lord, for my life. God, You gave me life and You continue to shower me with gifts. I pray what You have given me in abundance, I will share with those in need.

Lord, I reflect on forgiveness- that I have been forgiven and that I need to forgive. Thank you, Lord, for Your forgiveness and grace. During times of trial and stress, I know You understand and care because You have been there. I have hope that the difficult times will pass. With life everlasting, we are born anew into a world of joy, beauty, knowledge, acceptance and love. When I need to—-I can forgive then choose to stay or walk away. I can forgive while not allowing someone to hurt or take advantage again. Sometimes I need to forgive myself.

Lord, I reflect on the power of prayer and how I can help those in need. Lord, I pray for those who are ill and perhaps even close to death. It is not Your will that anyone suffer, however, tragedies and suffering are a reality in this chaotic world. When there are dark days of suffering I can choose to become a stronger and more empathetic person. Experiencing both good and bad situations matures my soul. Sometimes there are miracles and the power of prayer is awesome. There may also be times when I am an answer to someone's prayer. I pray for the caretakers of those with long term illness.

Lord, I reflect on the need for research, understanding of mental illness and the struggles that people and families go through on a daily basis. Lord, I pray for healing for those suffering from mental illness, depression, anxiety, addictions and emotional trauma. Lord, may they have hope to carry on while seeking the help of family, friends and professionals.

Lord, I reflect on my gratitude that there is food on the table for me and my family. I pray for adults and children that go to sleep hungry. I pray for financial healing. Poverty is a global disease that can be eliminated by the absence of greed, corruption, cultural bigotry and ignorance. No child should go to bed starving. It can be eliminated with education, equal rights, acceptance, affordable health care, hard work and people with helping hands.

Lord, I reflect on my need to know you better. Lord, most importantly, I pray for Spiritual Healing. People and countries are spiritually diseased, spiritually depressed, spiritually poor and spiritually hungry. Holy Spirit move from land to land and stir winds of curiosity to know a loving and saving God. Holy Spirit, move with the power of ocean waves to bring people to their knees in prayer and to look outside of themselves to You for answers.

I reflect in the name of Jesus that God's will be done. In all things there is hope–there is healing–there is joy. Amen

No Deep Thoughts Today

I don't always need deep thoughts or words to pray. At this moment I want to calmly relax and just enjoy being in Your presence.

Prayer of Warmth and Concern

Romans 8:28. Amen

In the coldness of this winter day, I am thankful for the warmth of Your love. I am also thankful that my body is warm and my basic needs are a reality. I pray for those who struggle to keep warm because they have no home or struggle just to survive.

If I choose to alleviate the inner pain, strife, heartaches, restless urges and angry moments; Christ's guidance will come to me.

If I will listen to the music Christ orchestrates for me- I will dance.

If I open my eyes to see- there will be an inner beauty within me.

I lift up a friend who walks a mile with me as we share tears and laughter along the way.

Although I can't untangle all the woes of someone I care about, with Your help, Lord, I can give a cup of support and a scoop of laughter to *(name)* lonely and grieving heart. I pray the Holy Spirit will guide us both.—

Lord, I am glad You are in my life. Amen

I Will Fly Like an Eagle

Isaiah 40:31

Response: *I will fly like an eagle!* Feel the energy. You can respond out loud or silently:

Even on a grey Winter day, Your creation is awesome. The winter landscape is like a Black and White photo or movie...beautiful in its own way... yet I know the Technicolor of Spring and Summer will arouse a new kind of beauty full of energy. As *I* daily gaze on Your creation

With the love of God in my heart... *I will fly like an eagle!*

I am thankful for every opportunity to worship You. Holy Spirit, I pray for Your inspiration and guidance through my life when I sing, pray and learn of God's majesty. I am thankful for musicians whose

faith urges them to musically express the joy of knowing Jesus Christ. When I hear Your music or sing a song
  With the love of God in my heart...*I will fly like an eagle!*

I pray for the community of Christians as we continue a legacy of empowering and enabling Christians to renew their commitment to serve You and the whole of Your creation...here, there and everywhere. As I serve the needs of others
  With the love of God in my heart...*I will fly like an eagle!*

Lord, I pray that the needs of my family will continue to be available. Thank You that we have much more than necessary to survive. I need to remember that the more I have, the more I am called to share. I know, I can share more than "stuff". I can share my time to pray, to sew, to make cookies, to listen, to make music, to teach, to administrate, to be a friend...or whatever You call me to do. When I share
  With the love of God in my heart...*I will fly like an eagle!*

Lord, I know You are with me during the difficult times. You are with me when I'm scared, when I'm angry (sometimes at You), when I'm tempted, or when I'm weary. There will often be times when I falter in the wind but in the end-
  With the love of God in my heart...*I will fly like an eagle!*

I lift up _____ for Your healing and the comfort You so willingly give.
  Whenever I pray for those near and dear with the love of God in my heart...*We will fly like an eagle*
  In the name of Jesus, Your will be done worldwide in all things with the love of God in peaceful hearts. Amen

Prayer Journey

This is a contemplative prayer in which you will be guided to pray your own thoughts to God. Before beginning the journey prepare for it by relaxing: sit comfortably–shoulders down -relax your abdomen and then your legs, feet and toes–hands on your knees with palms up– Breathe in slowly through your nose with the thought 'Yah' and then exhale slowly through your mouth with the thought 'wey'. (Yahweh is a name for God)

Come into my heart, Lord Jesus
Come into my soul, Holy Spirit
Come into my gut, God so I know You are real
I appreciate the beauty of Your creation
I am thankful for
I regret
Holy Spirit inspire me
I love You
Help me
I wonder

Take a deep breath in with the thought "thank" and then exhale with the thought "You'"

I Believe
Ephesians 1:17-19

Lord-
I believe that You are the one true god
I believe that You love me
I believe Your power and grace surrounds us all
I believe in the power of the Holy Spirit to change lives
I believe that You are smiling at Christian children throughout the world who express joy in knowing the God they love.

I believe that You are active in my life and want me to communicate with you every day

I believe in miracles

I believe You are paving the way for missionaries as they live and work touching lives and being touched. I share Your joy.

I believe that I am forgiven

I believe that I need to forgive

I believe that You answer prayer

I believe You are there for me in the midst of my storms. During them, I can say, " You are my God".

I believe You are there for me in my times of doubt

I believe You are there for me when I am afraid.

I believe in the healing power of prayer and I pray for your healing touch to—

I also pray for someone in my life who needs Your intervention

Some people believe that when they die, if they follow the light, they will see God. When we seek Your truth as we live, we can glance in wonder at God now.

May I be open to Your will at all times

Lord, Your will be done in all things- both near to me and of global impact. Amen

Thoughts on Prosperity
I Peter 1:4-5

Prelude: May today be all I need it to be. May the Peace of God and the freshness of the Holy Spirit rest in my thoughts, rule in my dreams and conquer all my fears.

May my joys be sustained, my dreams closer to being fulfilled and my prayers be answered according to Your will. I pray that my faith in a loving God reaches a new height. I pray my successes be increased. I pray for peace, healing, health, happiness, prosperity, joy, truth and an undying Love for God.(Continue each thought below in your own words to God.)

God of love, thank you for
Lord, help me to deal thoughtfully with
Holy Spirit guide my faith to
Lord, help me to reach outside of my comfort zone so that I
I pray that my family and I will prosper.
I will share my prosperity by
Even though I still miss them, I am glad my loved ones are with You
in a place beautiful beyond my comprehension.
God, thank you for all the blessings in my life. Amen

Love Is a Verb
I John 4:7

Selah means to stop & think. After the word, Selah, pause. –Then think about what you have just talked to God about or continue the prayer in your own words.

Good morning (or afternoon/evening) God. Thank You for each opportunity to praise You, learn more about who You are and to commune with You. I want to put a smile on Your face today... *Selah*

Father, there are traces of Your footsteps in everything. Help me to connect with the unity of all things and all people... *Selah*

Lord, I know You want real conversation...not just religious words. Holy Spirit, help me to be more comfortable as I feel Your presence when we talk through prayer... *Selah*

A dog knows <u>where</u> the tree is but it doesn't know <u>what </u>a tree is. People know. I know my creator had an idea and then there were trees. Many people can understand that You exist. You are so much more! You are a god of infinite love. Speaking of love- help me to love more kindly and help me to love with a passion that has fewer strings attached. May my love for You, my God, be less religious and more of a relationship. I want to love You with a commitment to be a BFF with You. I have much to learn about loving my family, friends and even those who are not all that lovable... *Selah*

Love is not a noun. Love is a verb. Love is not a thing, it is a relationship, God, I know You love me and want a relationship with me. Agape love should not be a sloppy passive love. Agape is a positive energy of goodness... *Selah*

Thank You, Jesus for the invitation to be baptized in Your name and to continue the relationship at the Communion table. I am sorry for my imperfect way of loving You and others. I am so glad You love me anyway.... *Selah*

God, please bless my family. I especially lift up to You ___*name*___

Help me to know You and love You more actively and fully....*Selah*

I pray, in Jesus's name, that Your love is known and accepted in every nook and cranny of God's creation. Amen.

Contemplative Prayer–In the Middle of the Ocean

– Relax, close your eyes for a moment and then take a deep breath. God does not need words—just think about your relationship with Him. Pause and reflect wherever in the prayer that you want to expand on.

Imagine you are sitting on a rock*, in the middle of an ocean,

The rock does not feel hard; it is very comfortable as your feet dangle in the ocean. Water is lapping gently, caressing your feet and ankles. The sky is blue as pure white clouds beckon to be touched as they leisurely shape shift to different images.

You sigh with contentment and of being surrounded by a peace that you don't totally understand. You are aware that the there is also a great power contained in the body of the ocean, which at this moment is a gentle giant.

God, You created this ocean that teems with abundant life. Awesome!

Every breath I take is known to You. Each tear I shed is understood.

If I decide to slide off of the rock—the safe place—the water will hold me if I don't panic. I just need to relax and float on my back. God, You are there when I take risks or there is change in my life. I can also choose to swim—to make good things happen in my life or to help others. There are times I need to pause in order to drink in the fullness of life and to ponder...or just to be grateful. There are times to float as I gently explore my options. There are times to acknowledge that I can't do it all alone. I need You, Lord. There are times when I need to be more than a bystander.

Thank you for the beauty and splendor surrounding me that is just a glimpse of what is yet to be seen and experienced.

I am open to life as the Holy Spirit leads me, guides me and motivates me.

I pray for my family and friends to have a relationship with You. I pray that Your Word flourishes as missionaries spread the gospel of Your love. I stand on that rock in the middle of the ocean with my arms wide open to accept Jesus as my Savior, God the Father as my creator and the Holy Spirit as my guide to a life of meaning and purpose. Lord, I want my faith and understanding to mature. I want to stay safely in tranquil and playful waters. When rough waters become dangerously close, I know You will be on the rock with me.

Amen to swimming with faith and purpose.

*I know rocks don't float, however, anything is possible with God and our imagination.

Rejoice, God Made Today
Psalm 118:12

Good morning, Lord. Thank You for the glory of today. I am glad to be sharing this day with You.

You are in the world and You are within me. Glory Hallelujah! As I prepare to wend my way on this day that You have made, I choose to shake the grumbles away and be a positive influence throughout my endeavors. I am content knowing I am imperfect because I am Your child still growing in Your care. I can rejoice within the frustration of coping with difficult circumstances because You will see me through them. I know You love me. Lord give me the wisdom to enjoy myself today and in any little way help someone else enjoy a moment.

Love You God! Amen

Footprints in the Sand
Revelation 22:1-2

Jesus sees my footprints in the sand as I walk along my life's shore. Jesus sees my footprints in the sand when challenging winds dump debris within and without my footprints. Jesus sees my footprints in the sand as incoming waves distort the firm outline of who I am and sometimes I am not exactly sure if those are my footprints in the sand. Jesus sees my footprints in the sand when people either intentionally or unintentionally trample on my essence. Jesus sees my footprints in the sand enjoying the walk as I wade in living waters. Jesus sees my footprints in the sand when they are no longer distinguishable to the human eye. Jesus sees my footprints in the sand as He walks beside me on the shore every day of this life. We will stroll together forever along a never-ending shoreline sharing beautiful moments along with a myriad other footprints. We will all be in harmony with the beauty of our surroundings. Holy Spirit, guide my walk along the shore.

Amen to my walk and to the walk of others...

Let My Soul Take Flight

Inspired by the book, the movie and the music of Jonathan Livingston Seagull. Think about who you think Skybird is. Is it you, something that is within you or someone else reaching out to you?

Jonathan Livingston Seagull are you real or are you taking flight in my mind? Skybird, you are telling me to crest the waves sweetly.

Songbird, I want to rejoice in you and myself...To take flight in the possible because for us dreams are reality.

Hallelujah, the distant shores are reached. Perhaps with pain; but touched in joy on silver wings. The children's chorus is singing for life to be lived in harmony and the peace of stillness.

Death becomes the crescendo of the unlost, hazy dreamer to a life not of stone and bones and silence. But to a new song of fulfillment and windy days in which to take flight amidst violins. Let me live! So that I may live the dreams of love and enjoy the snow that does not chill.

Dreamer, dream your dreams and do not fear to awake and pluck your soul where you are. Do not wait to bloom or you will be lonely waiting. Waiting while the frost nips the bud; never to blossom.

Skybird, take flight from those who desire to stifle you into conformity. Flying in freedom is a wondrous thing but it can be lonely in your independence- till you fully understand and meet another willing to spread the wings of freedom to the distant shore. Another bird in flight in a different motion. Now you are not quite alone in your loneliness.

Loneliness is not sadness. It just is. The independence of it allows me to be the best of me without fear of rejection. I know there are some who do smile on my flight and even more awesome are those who fly higher than I have yet flown. Take flight. Take flight with the spirit in the sky.

My Strength–My Heart–My Hero

Inspired by the song, *The Wind Beneath My Wings* by Larry Henley/Jeff Silbar) Matthew 7:7

Dear God, You are my hero. I think in wonder of all that You really are. Knowing You enhances every aspect of my life. As I pray, walk, run and fly through my days, You are within my surroundings and at the same time within my core being. Because You are the wind beneath my wings, I can sometimes fly beyond the superficial. I can soar to new heights of understanding my purpose and the meaning of the universe.

It is good when people praise Your children for the talents they share. We all appreciate gold stars sprinkled here and there. A missionary knows their call is from God to serve and sometimes in risky or uncomfortable places. Holy Spirit, lead me and encourage me to be a blessing with whatever talent I have...music, listening with empathy, teaching, leading, crafting, feeding, visiting, writing, counseling, healing, preaching, praying and loving to name a few. Jesus, You were the one with all the strength as You lived and prepared for Your destiny on the cross. Never once did you complain. Not my will but Your will be done with me. Whatever we do in Your name for Your purpose we do more eloquently as we fly above the wind of Your strength.

Oh, God, You are in my heart. I know I often take You for granted. I know I still have questions and I don't have it all together or have all right answers. I don't even ask all the right questions. I am still searching but I've got You in my heart. I dread to think what my life would be like without You. But I don't have to fear because You are as close as the beating of my heart.

Lord, be the wind beneath the wings of_____

Amen

THE LORD'S PRAYER

The Lord's Prayer–You are Everything

The Lord's Prayer is more than a prayer to be memorized and said by rote. It is a guide for us on how to communicate to God. Christians can prayerfully use our own words to express our feelings and needs to God. You can pause at any place in the prayer to meditate or expand your thoughts in your own words. The following five prayers are different renditions of the Lord's Prayer.

Father-

You are in all of Your creation. Your presence is all around me and within me

Your name is holy. How You must wince each time You hear Your name uttered without respect and especially in an angry curse. I pray my thoughts and musings are positive. I pray my words are uplifting and my actions productive. I pray I do Your will at home, at work or wherever I am. I look forward to doing Your will when I return to my eternal home with You and my loved ones.

Lord, please continue to sustain me with food and drink for my body and my soul. Thank You so much for richness in my life. There are so many conveniences that I take for granted. Thank You for the miracles and the incredible coincidences to be at the right place and at the right time. You bless my life in so many ways every day. Thank You.

Thank You, Father, for loving me and forgiving me. I pray that I can also forgive hurtful words and actions without allowing them to hurt me again.

Lord, give me the will and insight to make the right choices in life. I want to choose goodness and kindness.

I pray for peace. Deliver humanity from acts of hatred and war. I pray for the victims of Domestic Violence; the victims of Political Injustice; the victims of natural disasters and the victims I have hurt along the way with my words, actions or silence.

The universe is Yours. Your power is awesomely unimaginable and Your glory outshines the darkness. May the holy Spirit lead me to Your light. Thank You for sharing Your love to infinity.

I love you. Amen

Lord's Prayer Past, Present and Future

My God of the past, present and future. You are a Father of love and justice to all humanity. I am blessed to be Your child.

I'm sorry for the disrespectful use of Your holy name which signifies how much You are taken for granted in our so called modern world. You have told us over and over how you expect Your children to respect who You are and to use Your name ONLY with the respect it is due.—just as any loving parent expects their children to do the same.

The place You live is real. You live both without and within me. May it be real to me as I go about my daily business. I pray for glimpses of clarity of what Your kingdom is like for me when I spend alone time with You.

Lord, help me to understand the difference between Your will, my will and the events that happen in a world of free will. We tend to think in the present of our life on earth. You think beyond the present to a forever life with You. You clearly see the big picture. My view is limited and cloudy.

Oh Lord, help me to do Your will by responding in love to children around the world who are starving for food, education, affection or the hope that You give so freely. I appreciate that I have more than I need to survive in this world.

I don't want to forget or take for granted *the great Sacrifice-the great Forgive*. I need to forgive and forgive again and again if that is what is needed. Anger and bitterness tear me down instead of lifting me up.

Temptations are around every corner and world news overflows with violence, injustice and false values. Lord, please help me to stay on the right path as I continue my relationship with You and my faith and knowledge of Your truth matures.

The power of Your love is awesome. I want to dwell in that love forever. Amen

The Lord's Prayer -Father of All Humanity

Dear Father of all humanity: Heaven is all around and within all of us. You are the loving creator of people with physical and mental challenges. You are the god of people I have disagreements and conflicts with.

I know Your name is holy. You must wince hearing the flippant way we speak Your name. I am sorry for the times I am disrespectful. Sometimes I just don't think before I speak when using Your name.

Your kingdom is here and a place beyond our knowledge. It is a place even more beautiful than the brightest rainbow. It is a place I want to continue my forever journey to my forever home. Thank You for the stuff I take for granted. Please give us food and drink for our bodies and souls. Thank You for the miracles in my life and the incredible coincidences to be at the right place at the right time. I will share my blessings. Thank You so much for forgiving my hurtful words, dark thoughts and destructive actions. I pray that I can forgive the relatively insignificant and the seemingly unforgiveable actions of others without allowing them to cause pain again. Lord, give me the will and insight to make the right choices in life. I will choose to express goodness and kindness in my interactions with others. I know you want peace and harmony... Let it begin with me. Help me to listen in silence in order to know that it is You, God, whispering to my heart. You do hear my prayers but sometimes I'm not still enough to hear Your answer. Deliver us all from acts of hatred, violence, addictions, corruption and spiteful acts. God, Your glory outshines the darkness. The universe is Yours and Your power is awesomely unimaginable. The power of Your love can move mountains of doubt, depression, oppression and apathy. Your kingdom is complete harmony. Thank You for sharing Your love forever into eternity. I love you! Amen

The Lord's Prayer–You are the One

Contributed by Sue Hosler

Our Father, creator of all humanity, yet <u>my</u> loving father- You are the one "who knit me together in my mother's womb," as the psalmist, David, declared. You know me inside and out. Though You are in heaven, You are at the same time right beside me guiding my footsteps.

Your name is holy and commands respect. Guard my lips against using it in a disrespectful way. When I hear Your name profaned in any way as I go about my day, may I utter a counter prayer praising Your name.

May Your kingdom come in the lives of each of us, Your children. Help me to emulate the life of Jesus, who showed us that Your kingdom comes through loving one another with deeds of mercy, kindness and compassion. Though You give us free will, may I strive to seek Your will that it may be done in ways that create the highest good in the lives of others.

Provide for the daily needs that sustain our lives and give us a confidence that we need not worry about tomorrow for we can trust in Your providential care always.

Forgive me for the sinful things I have done and free me from the guilt of things I have left undone. Mend the cracked and broken pieces of my life and bless me with the joy of Your salvation. As You are merciful and forgiving to me, may I forgive those who treat me wrongly. Remove hurt, anger, bitterness, pride or sorrow and any desire for revenge. Replace it with a grace filled spirit.

Hold me back from engaging in sinful behavior as I am confronted with temptation both from the world around me and ungodly thoughts and desires within me. May Your Holy Spirit speak to me and give me strength to resist temptations and guide me in the paths of righteousness.

Hear our cries for protection against the evil in our world, especially for the inhumanity perpetrated against one another, which causes deep sorrow and distress in our hearts. Give us renewed hearts of love and peace. We look with confident hope towards life eternal with You where there will be no more death or mourning or crying or pain, for those things will have passed away.

Your kingdom endures forever. You are worthy of glory, honor and power for You created the whole universe and everything in it. You continue to sustain it and we acknowledge Your great and marvelous deeds as You actively work in our world and our lives. Praise, love and thanksgiving unto to You, O Lord and King of our lives. Amen-let it be so!

PRAYERS TO LIVE BY

Muddy Waters

I am here God reaching out to You. I feel Your presence and I smile as I think of the goodness of You that is part of me. Sometimes I need to focus on the better part of me just as sometimes I need to work on some of my issues and hang-ups. The more I know Jesus, the better I know myself and I can feel confident that I am spiritually growing up. Lord, at this moment I feel the energy of Your love and acceptance. I want to walk to the well of Your living water. The water from Your well is clear and quenches the thirst in my soul. I would not drink a glass of dirty water. So, why would I want my soul to drink a cup of muddy water tainted with harmful organisms like anger, greed, gossip, negativity, trashy media, violence, apathy and whatever puts distance between You and me? Holy Spirit, thank You for guiding me to the clear waters of goodness and love. Thank You for leading me to the message and persona of Jesus Christ. Thank You, Jesus for showing the way to transform the muddy waters in my life to crystal clear waters that fill me up with God's presence.

I will drink up and enjoy life ! Amen

Plucking the Thorns
II Corinthians 12:7-10 Mark 4:7

God, because You are so awesome in Your fairness, I do not have to be afraid of You. I do not need to be afraid of where You will lead me.

I respect the precision of Your creation. I am so sorry mankind has screwed it up in so many ways. Sometimes by corporations and developers with intentional greed; sometimes with inconsiderate pollution, littering or an apathy to repurposing because it is inconvenient. Let recycling be a priority worldwide, within my community, and let it begin with me. After all, the earth is my home prepared by You, God. Will we also litter the new mansions?

Thank You, God, for serendipitous moments that make my day. Are they a coincidence or a smile and a wink from You?

When difficult times challenge my spirit, help me to become stronger, more empathetic and closer to You.

My words and actions have a ripple effect on others–both positive and negative. Holy Spirit, help me to always spread more positive than negative vibes. May I learn from my mistakes and poor decisions.

Part of my spiritual journey is to remove the thorns in my essence. Thorns that when touched, cause me emotional cause me emotional pain, resentment, guilt, self righteousness, withdrawal or sometimes explosive reactions. Holy Spirit, help me to be aware of the thorns stunting my relationships and my spiritual journey. Help me to learn from them and to pluck them from my soul.

Thank You for my friends who encourage, help and support me. Jesus, for the opportunity to remember You while participating in Holy Communion. It keeps You alive in our souls.

I pray for peace wherever there is conflict. I pray for safe spaces for those who need them. May those who grieve know their loved one is transformed to a new life. In the name of Jesus, Your will be done on the seas, in the desert and in urban communities.

In the name of Jesus, Your will be done as mission teams shine in Your love while sharing the good news of Jesus. May all the obstacles to the mission be removed for a successful mission ending with their safe return.

Love you! Amen

Dreams for Fulfillment

Complete the unfinished portions of the prayer with your own thoughts to God.

My God of Peace, You are more than I need You to be. Thank You! May the freshness of the Holy Spirit's truth rest in my thoughts, rule in my dreams tonight and conquer all my fears. I pray You manifest Yourself to me and others in ways we have not experienced before. May my joys be realized, my dreams drift closer to fulfillment and my prayers be answered. I pray that my faith continues to reach for a clearer understanding of Your presence within me and the world. I pray for peace, healing, health, happiness, prosperity and joy along with a true and undying Love for God.

God of love, thank You for
Lord, help me to deal thoughtfully with
Holy Spirit, guide those to whom God is unknown to them
Inspire my journey of faith
Lord, help me to reach outside of my comfort zone so that I
I pray that my family and I will prosper
I will share my prosperity by
Even though I still miss them, I am glad my loved ones are with You in a beautiful beyond my comprehension place.
I pray for Your healing and comfort to ......
God, thank You for all the blessings in my life. Amen

Happy Spring

It is a wonderful day to worship You, Lord. Yesterday, as the world turned- Spring peeked around the corner. The Spring bulbs stretching toward the sky from the earth reminds me that my Savior lives. My Savior lives! Gloria Hallelujah! I offer up to You the needs of those in distress so that they can appreciate Spring days with a smile. I pray Your will be done for ...name.....

Glory to You, God, as an integral part of the universe and of being within my soul. Love You. Amen

Beacon of Faith
Philippians 4:13

God of heaven and earth. You are the greatest!!! You are so awesome; yet, it is so nice that I can just talk with You about anything and know You are listening. Help me to become a beacon of faith and kindness as I share Your love with the people in my life. As I share, I will catch glimpses of the heaven (future) You are preparing for me. Holy Spirit, guide me as I prepare for that journey throughout my life. Holy Spirit guide me when I ask difficult questions, have doubts or when I need to make decisions that affect my life and the lives of others. (It is not just about me) What we seek is what we are. When I connect with my God who is always dwelling in me, I will find my true self. I can have power in my life since Christ is in me and I can make good things happen. Holy Spirit, direct me to be a good steward of Your gifts to me. I need to pay attention when You call me to use those gifts.

(Take a deep breath and pause in silence.)
God is good. Amen

Help Me to Grow in Faith
Romans 8:38-39 John 6:26-27

Lord of all things created; please accept my praise and prayer. I pray that I am open to the Holy Spirit when I meditate on Your word and Your purpose for me. Thank You for loving me more than I love myself. Thank You for accepting and understanding me as I am. Help me to grow in Your love as I go about the daily activities that take up so much of my time. Holy Spirit, help me with tough questions and my doubts so that my faith in You becomes more real to me in 'The Knowing' that God is within me. I pray that when I am faced with difficult times, the journey through them will make me a stronger soul. I can cope with anything with You at my side.

Thank You for Your mercy and grace. I am sorry when my reluctance to living harmoniously has caused hurt feelings to others. I also need to be a positive role model for those who disregard the well being of the planet we call home. I pray for peace throughout the world. I pray for friendships to remain loyal and true. I pray for new understanding between people of different countries and cultures as people experience getting to know people from diverse backgrounds. As a Child of God, place me in the right time and place to help someone in both big and small ways. Help me to remember that a smile of acceptance can make a person's day or that a positive remark to a child can have a lasting or even a life changing affect. In the name of Jesus, Your will be done in all things Amen

Go Team!

God, I know You don't take sides in sports. It really isn't fair to put You in the middle because fans on both sides are praying for a win. I'm old enough to remember when the Cleveland Browns and Indians were a dominate forces in the national sport scene. Gone are the days of Paul Brown, Bill Veeck and the original Barons. I have a confession to make. Since Cleveland has been the underdog for more than a decade I have asked for some interventions and maybe a miracle or two. How interesting it is that people are afraid of being religious fanatics but will put on cheesy hats, dawg masks and an abundance of cumbersome paraphernalia while hooting, barking, making waves and stomping while tailgating and attending games.

Whether it be Little League, scholastic or professional sports, I pray for sportsmanship among coaches, players, parents and fans. I pray players strive for the positive values of team work, commitment and hard work. I pray coaches and players be a positive role model both on the field and in their community.

When the games begin, Your will be done in the hearts of all who participate and those who watch in the bleachers. Amen

Knock Knock Who's There?
Revelation 3:20

Knock Knock
Who's there?
God
God Who?
God who loves you. May I please come in to your life?

Thinking Positive Today
Isaiah 44:22

Father, You are not God of Gods. You are the only God. It is only You that I can put my complete trust in. The more I trust You the more I will follow Your guidance to a fulfilling life. You give me so much and only ask that I respect You and live in harmony with my surroundings. Lord, help me to understand that when I sin I turn my back on You. Negative actions, thoughts and words are symptoms of turning our backs on You and Your values. Help me to live a more harmonious life in tune to Your will. I am so fortunate that Jesus welcomes sinners because that would be me. Thank You for the gift of today. I will open it with excitement. Lord, I decide to be happy and positive today. With Your help, I will accept change as an adventure. I will accept the losses in my life as an education and an opportunity to open new doors. Father, Son and Holy Spirit; it is a joy getting to know You. Amen

Growing in Love
Lamentations 3:22-23

Thank you, God, for loving me more than I love myself. Thank you for accepting and understanding me as I am. Help me to grow in Your love as I go about the daily activities that take up so much of my time. Help me with my tough questions and my doubts so that my faith in You becomes more real to me. I pray that when I am faced with difficult times, the journey through them will make me a stronger person. I can deal with anything with You at my side. I confess that I have sinned against You and many others. I am sorry for the hurts I have caused others to feel. Thank You for Your forgiveness and grace. Lord, there is someone I care about who needs You. I pray for_____

You are a mystery and I am curious to know more about You, however, I don't need to have all the answers to feel Your truth and love. I love You too! Amen

Love Blooms
Ephesians 2:10

Lord God, You are the creator of all existence. We live in an awesome world surrounded by beauty... A beauty even more radiant as warming weather encourages flowers and trees to once again embrace Your land with color. You created life- my life. Because of my Savior, my life is never ending. You created my soul and You sustain my soul. In You, Christ, I am a new creation. Help me to let loose my love for You and let go of the weeds that strangle a purpose filled life. Like the flowers in a garden I want my soul to bloom and I also want to be like the bee, butterfly or hummingbird that pollinates other souls with the nectar of faith. With the help of the Holy Spirit I want to bloom with the colors of love, kindness, helpfulness, caring and empathy. I want to share my faith in a loving god who nourishes the love blossoms of all the varieties of humankind.

Lord, give me a tender heart that lets me say and do loving and compassionate things, which surprise even myself. Amen

Great God of Love
I Corinthians 13:1-3

Great God of love- who gives so abundantly. Your love covers the earth warming hearts and encouraging timid souls to soar. Lord, I long to love You more boldly. I pray the Holy Spirit will help me to grow in Your love and to love others in the way that You have shown us to love. I pray people will make decisions and choices that will be a positive force in the community. Lead our minds and hearts to make bold decisions to serve You, our God. I am thankful for the many people who give of their time in service to help others and who make a difference in the gardens where they are planted. I am sorry for my sins- for what I have thought, for what I have done and for what I have ignored. With Your help, I can resist the temptations that haunt me. Lord, help me with-(*continue* in your own words)

Lord, lead me to Your will and the manner I can serve You in the various areas of my life. Lord, I pray for someone in my life that needs to be touched by the Holy Spirit. Thank You for being You! In the name of Jesus, hear my prayer. Amen

Dancing With God
Psalm 46:6-7

Lord, thank You for this Gorgeous day. It is good to be alive and talking with You. Sometimes music makes me want to get up and dance. Doing Your will is a lot like dancing. When both dancers try to lead, nothing feels quite right. The movement doesn't flow with the music. When one of the dancers realizes that the other must lead, both bodies begin to flow with the music as one gives gentle cues or a nudge to the back. The dance takes surrender, willingness and attentiveness to the leader. When I allow You Lord, to be my leader, I can dance to any music that life brings on. I pray that people dance with You as their leader to guide them through each season of our lives. Lord help me to keep my words soft and sweet so I won't have to eat them and to keep both feet out of my mouth at the same time. I need one leg to stand on. Lord, I need to take time to be silent this week and to take time to just let You know what is in my heart. Then I will listen to the music You have prepared for me. In the name of Jesus, I will dance with joy! Amen

Come Into My Heart
John 8: 12

Lord, come into my heart today as I worship You in prayer, thanks-giving and in Communion with Your word. Your word is truth, light and life. I pray that my family and I be drawn to the light of Your word so that we can then help to share the truth of Your love to others. It is encouraging to experience the light of knowing You casting hope in the dark places of my life. Help me to continue, throughout my life, to live in harmony with Your will, in harmony with others and in harmony with myself. I know I am not perfect. I also know that You are not through with me yet. Thank You for the many miracles in my life. In all things, Your will be done. AMEN

Prayer of Harmony
Philippians 4: 6-7

Dear God- Father of Life- Who is in all life- I praise You because there is power to my Spirit in praise. There is apathy in disrespect. I come to You in awe and respect. Help me not to take You and Your gifts of love, forgiveness and miracles for granted. I pray the world matures in harmony as You intended it to be. I pray people will be motivated to do their part in kindness and a resolve to make life better for someone else. Holy Spirit, guide people to give their time and resources for others. Help us to teach our children harmony and sharing. I look forward to being in perfect harmony of everlasting life in Your presence. I pray for reconciliation and understanding within families where resentment is harbored. I pray for harmony within myself so that I can be a blessing to others and to You. Yep, even to myself. I want never to turn my back on You, my God. Instead, I want to be caught in Your open arms of love and acceptance. Thank you for being such a loving God. Amen

Meeting God at the Pearly Gates

If I were interviewed: "What would I want God to say to me when I enter the pearly gates?" Would I say; God doesn't need to say anything. I just want to see His open arms welcoming me to my Eternal Home...or what would I want to hear from God?

Lord, guide me to be open and accepting of Your message in the Word. Our lives and minds are bombarded by so much garbage in a culture of instant technology and instant gratification. We need to be refreshed with pure thoughts and more positive energy. Too many children are immersed in negative lyrics and angry sounding music. I pray their minds and souls be more attracted to positive images and messages. I need to make better choices about what I watch, what I hear and what I read. *Garbage in, garbage out.* Parents tell their children that "just because everyone else is doing it; that doesn't make it right". Adults need to say the same thing to themselves. I need to say it to myself. Lord, help me to know the difference between cultural values and Your values. Lord, You are not only my Savior, my God; You are my friend- my best friend. I want to talk with You as comfortably and as candidly as a good friend. You know my dark places. You love me and accept me as I am. I have nothing to fear or hide from You. I want to talk with You so that my prayers are real rather than by rote. It is a process and I will work on communicating with You more often. Love You, Jesus Amen

I'll Do It Your Way
Romans 3:19-28

My God, You are the creator of all worlds and universes. How You did it, I don't know- but I do know Your creative hand still touches the land and life of this earth we call home. When I say, "Your name is holy" in the Lord's Prayer, I need to remember to not use Your name in an irreverent way. No excuses. For the love of God, I'll do it Your way. Is it time to move on to a more meaningful relationship with You? Positive change is vital for growth. God, I ask for inspiration to enlighten and strengthen my faith in You. For the love of God, I'll reform to Your way. Lord, I pray for Peace. Let it begin with me as I interact with my family, friends, schoolmates and co-workers. For the love of God, I'll do it Your way.

Thank you for the breath I take, the food so readily available and for the opportunity to Commune at Your table as a forgiven child of God. I am sorry for the times my words and actions have hurt others. I regret choices that have distanced me from those I love- including You. For the love of God, I want to do it Your way by building people up rather than tearing them down. Lord, I pray for caretakers who respond to the needs of the vulnerable who are struggling with illness, dementia, addictions, depression, grief or isolation. Holy Spirit, fill their hearts with patience, good will and a positive attitude. I pray the experience strengthens the faith of both the caregiver and those they are caring for. For the love of God, help caregivers to do it Your way with empathy and compassion. Lord, I pray for truth that allows souls to soar. I pray that I accept Your truth and where needed, to embrace a reformation in my life. I will dance in my mind to a beat of joy, caring and the love of God to do it Your way. In the name of Jesus, I pray that humanity will live with purpose to serve by doing it Your way. Amen

Fill Up With God
I John 4:7

Dear God, I am so in awe of Your greatness and goodness. Thank You for Your generosity that allows me to be alive and live in Your presence. With Jesus there is always Hope, Strength and Courage to go on regardless of my circumstances. Thank You for my friends who encourage, help and support me. Please bless their lives. Jesus, You didn't die so I can have a religion and go to church on Sunday. You suffered till death so I can have a relationship with You- a relationship for all eternity. Holy Spirit, fill my mind and soul full of God. Lift my spiritual essence to a higher level in communion with You. I pray Your will be done on earth and within me. Amen

God is the Potter of my Soul
Psalm 61: 1-

God, You are awesome and I am so glad to know You. I am the clay and You are the potter. I want to be clay that is pliable to Your will but there are times when I am too dry to feel the spirit; too unbending in my need to be in control; too mushy to be formed in Your will. Holy Spirit give me the will and courage to listen and act on Your purpose for me. Lord, be with those who are grieving. Help them to be comforted in knowing that their loved ones are more alive than ever while smiling in the face of God. I pray for_____. In the name of Jesus, I pray Your will blends with mine as I go about my daily routine and mingle with people from all walks of life. Your love makes me smile. Holy Spirit, sometimes I need to get the dust off of my light bulb of faith so I can shine more brightly. Sometimes I wonder who You are and how You came to be so awesome. Sometimes I wonder where You are.—within me? —out in space somewhere? or everywhere? Sometimes I wonder how much You have been hurt...by my ancestors, by Christians, non Christians and by me....yet You continue to give, bless and love us all. I am honored to experience Holy Communion when I attend worship and remember Your promise to be with us always. I confess that I often fall short of being the kind of person I should be. It is nice to know You love and forgive me anyway. I don't want to go to Heaven by myself. I want to share the good news. I pray for peace. Peace in homes. Peace in the streets. Peace in hospitals. Peace in the Middle East and other warring countries. Peace within. Thank You, God: that I exist–for warm water–for babies–for trees–for my friends–for soap–for chocolate–for flush toilets–for books and for loving me. In the name of Jesus, I pray the will of our Father be accomplished in all things and that I be clay formed into a vessel of Your love. Amen

God's Love Warms Me On a Winter Day
John 13: 35

Lord. Your love warms me on this cold winter day. Thank You for being such a caring God who continues to be committed to Your creation.

I am grateful for the never ending gifts You shower on my family and land on me. I am proud to be a follower of Christ. Holy Spirit, guide me to walk across any room, any place or in any situation as a Child of God to connect with and befriend another human being. I don't have to preach, plead, lecture or defend my faith in You. I want to walk the faith as a caring Christian empowered by Your love and salvation. Holy Spirit help me to do that.

I confess that I have a long way to go as I sin in thought and behavior. I know I am not perfect but You are not through with me yet.

In the name of Jesus, the will of God be done in the hearts of men and women.

AMEN

OMG–*One Magnificent God*
James 2: 1-17

Great God of the universe–Loving Savior of mankind–Spiritual guide to the truth–I appreciate Your presence in my life. God, You are awesome. I want to praise and honor You by only using Your name with respect. I wonder how You feel when you hear OMG? I know I wouldn't like my name or my earthly father's name being used with such disrespect or to cuss at someone. When I hear OMG I will now think One Magnificent God. Lord, I am thankful for the spiritual learning at my church as I gather with other Christians to hear and discuss our faith in You. I pray for the presence and motivation of the Holy Spirit to energize and inspire teachers and leaders. May we all be inspired by the stories and lessons taught in scripture. Help me to understand my purpose to serve others in Your name. I am thankful for opportunities to honor people in need by giving of my time, talents and funds. Instead of being judgmental, I want to love my neighbor as myself. Not an easy task but worth pursuing! Let mercy triumph over judgment in my life, in my community and everywhere. Help me to accept people as they are from the inside instead of how they look; what they wear or the stuff they have. Lord, I pray the United States of America as, 'One Nation Under God', remains strong in principles, unified in purpose and committed to peace.

I pray for religious staff as they teach, preach, type, clean, make music and share their faith in the community. I pray for church Council members, Elders and all the volunteers who share the vision of a church who cares and gives to the community as well as sharing the Good News of God's love and the saving grace of Jesus Christ. I pray for the healing of minds, bodies and souls. Let your presence be felt to _____ Thank You, for the many blessings in my life. Thank you for my family. Please keep us all safe from the danger of disasters, human mischief and our own temptations. In the name of Jesus, I pray Your will be done. Amen

Thank You for Jesus
Genesis 1: 1-31

Father, You have shown us Your love by sending Your son, with whom You are so proud. How mixed Your emotions must have been when Jesus was born because You knew what was ahead for Him. Thank You, thank You God for such a precious gift. You have the unimaginable power of creating the universe and giving the breath of life to all living creatures. The only thing that surpasses Your power is Your love. With all His power, Your son was not a tyrant. Instead, He came to serve and to save. I don't have to be afraid to get close because You are so approachable. I can tell You anything. I am so thankful, Holy Spirit, that You dwell among us to guide (not enforce) us to grow in truth and knowledge so that we can know our purpose and put our purpose into action. We don't have to be smart to know Your will. We just need to be open to your loving ways for what You ask of us is not a burden. Lord, bless my church family as we worship and serve You,. I pray that our lives be enriched and our faith multiplies. Holy Spirit, I pray that we will be amazed as You join with our youth to lead another generation into a relationship with an awesome God. Thank You for Jesus! Amen

God Is My Sunshine
Psalm 84: 11-12

This prayer is inspired by the song, You are My Sunshine, which was one of my favorites as a child and it is a special song I sing to my grandchildren incorporating their names into the lyrics.

Oh God, You are my sunshine. The source of all sunshine. You make me happy when skies are grey. I really don't know, Lord how much You love me. Please don't let temptations and doubts take my sunshine away. Lord, You said we are created in Your image. If so, then when You gave us a sense of humor, You should have a sense of humor too. We tend to bond to people who make us laugh and add mirth to our lives. Lord, help me to share my fun side with You and to appreciate that You also like to smile. Lord, I will share a smile and a laugh with You this week and hope it turns into a habit. Lord, I am thankful that the people dear to me who have passed on are with You. I miss them but I don't have to worry about them because they are standing in the radiance of Your sunshine. May the lessons they taught me stay with me. I pray for the young adults of today. Holy Spirit, guide them throughout their lives and keep them safe from spiritual predators who try to shake their faith in You. Give them spiritual mentors when they need someone to stand in the rays of Your sunshine with them. Lord, help me to be sensitive to the needs of others. Remind me to do Your will- even if it means only to listen to someone or give a word of encouragement. In all things Your will be done. Thank You for being my sunshine. Amen

If this prayer is used in a worship setting, someone can sing the song, You Are My Sunshine ,prior to the prayer and or just the refrain, You are my Sunshine. after each petition.

Thanks for Listening
Luke 10:20 Mark 12:41-44

God, creator of all things. You give so much and keep on giving and giving and giving. Thank You! Jesus, You told us to "Rejoice that our name is written in Heaven". If only I could really trust this, it would change my whole life agenda. Holy Spirit I am open to hearing the sparks of God's truth. Lord, I pray my faith in You matures. Holy Spirit, help me to know in the innermost core of my being that we are inseparable because You are part of me and we will always be together. I am thankful for my church which has given me the foundation of my faith and knowledge of You. My faith journey however, does not depend on the tassels and ribbons of religious accessories and theologies. My journey is also right now as I am spending time alone with You. Thanks for listening. I will also listen as I wend my way in this life and journey into the next. I know that even in the lean times, there will be enough bread and olive oil for my family to survive another day. I also pray that whether I live with abundance or poverty, I will share with those who have less. I pray Your healing, grace and comfort wrap around _____ In Jesus name, I pray that Your will be done in all things. Amen

God's Masterpiece
Song of Solomon 4: 16

I believe as I pray to You this day. I believe in the glory of Your creation as I hear the chirp of a cardinal, the flutter of leaves in the breeze or the soothing music of waves lapping toward the shore. I believe as I gaze at Your creative masterpieces- the simple elegance of a tree, flowers in bloom, shifting cumulus clouds drawing pictures in the sky and the smiling eyes of a child.

Thank You Lord, for such a beautiful creation! I will do my part to take care of it. I believe I am created in Your image- so help me to love more unconditionally; to forgive more freely and to share my laughter with You. I want to include You when I do something silly or my (child or pet) does the unexpected. I know You want me to be 'real' and myself with You. That takes practice because I respect You so much. Help me to have patience with my children- whether they be 2 or 42. Help me to be patient with my parents- whether they be 32 or 92. Holy Spirit, guide me to plant seeds of patience, faith, love and hope, so that I bloom wherever I am planted. Holy Spirit, I pray for Insight and Wisdom to be with clergy as they minister to their congregations and communities. I pray that the Holy Spirit inspires and clarifies those who pray and that we listen to the voice of God as we pray. Lord, I pray the Holy Spirit gives clarity of truth to_____. In all matters, I pray in the name of Jesus that God's will be done. Amen

Jesus, My Teacher
Mark 1:21-28

My God, You are god of the living both in this world and the next. I am forever grateful that You are involved in my life and I look forward to spending time with You in the next. I have a lot of questions. Jesus, You are not only my savior, You are a great teacher. You showed mankind the path to a productive life. You taught us to cope in the darkest of times and to make the most of our successes. Thank you, Jesus! I don't always take Your advice or heed Your teaching but I'm working on it. Holy Spirit help me to listen, understand and live in tune to loving relationships- especially my relationship with You. I need to give up my need to control what I think is right. Instead, I will try allowing Your truth to flow within me. Holy Spirit, guide me to teach others as I wend my way through each day. I teach by the way I live. I teach by the way I talk. Jesus taught me to respect Him, myself and others. To teach respect, I have to be respectful. Thank You for the beautiful people in my life that support my efforts and mentor me to be a better person. You did really good creating the animals that share my yard and home....well, there are a few that I would appreciate more if they were burrowing in a field a mile away. In all things and in all places, Your will be done. I hope to live my life doing Your will. Amen

Waiting for Spring
Matthew 5: 44-46

Lord, You bring light, to my life. You give me hope when I think my life is dull.. I do not have a clue, Lord, how much You love me. I need to think on this as I imagine Your cross of love. As I wait patiently, or not so patiently, for Spring, please give me a sense of humor to pass the days with my friends, coworkers and family. Let me pass on the joy of knowing You to those who need Your grace. Holy Spirit, help me to understand the purpose of my life and then to act accordingly to Your will. I am sorry for the times I have turned my back on You when making decisions that have hurt me or someone else. Sometimes I am just caught in muck and mire. I am so thankful for Your understanding and grace to erase my sin. Lord, give me the desire to know You better. Sometimes all it takes is to be quiet for a little while.

Lord, help me to mend a troubled relationship with_____ _____. I am thankful that the soul of every living thing is in Your hands. Help me to be Your partner in preserving the earth and all the beautiful critters and blossoms of Your creation. In all things, Your will be done Amen

WIDE OPEN SPACES

Get comfortable and relax. Slowly breathe in deeply through your nose and then exhale from your mouth. Gently push busy thoughts from your mind. Imagine standing on the pinnacle of a large rock formation. Your arms are open wide with fingers spread. As you gaze around, you see a skyline of rock formations and space. Lots of space. There is space between the sun drenched clouds that are shifting in slow motion to sculpt fanciful animals that drift into oblivion. I am comfortably warm while gentle breezes skim my face and arms.

What I am most aware of is space. I imagine God within all the space. God is in the air surrounding me and through the whole canyon. God is in all of the unending sky. At this moment I am sharing this immense space with God. This makes me feel_____.
I am aware of the vastness of God's presence. Awesome! I am just a pebble in the landscape, however, God knows me, loves me and wants to share space with me. As I sit on my imaginary rocky precipice I feel God's presence stirring my soul deep in my core. Thank you God for all that You are. I feel so secure in Your absolute love. Ahhh, I'm feeling good.

PRAYERS WITH A FOCUS ON PURPOSE

Your Will Be Done With Me
Revelations 3:20

Lord, I need to think when You knock on the door to my soul. When You do knock, will I answer? I want to open my mind and my soul to be one with You. Sometimes it is so hard to let go of my ego and my need to be in control. Sometimes I am afraid of what You will ask me to do. Sometimes I don't want to change my way of thinking because I am comfortable with my faith and don't want to rock my beliefs with challenging questions. Do I even know what I believe or who I think You are? Dare I even question what I have learned over the years? As long as I'm in the playing field I want to be a spiritual athlete who leaves a legacy of faith. I am thankful for my ancestors who paved paths of faith. Because of them, my own faith is on more solid ground and my spiritual journey has fewer rocks and puddles in the road. I lift up with fond memories those who have said farewell to this life. Transformed, they exist now with a bright forever future. I lift up my family and friends, especially _____ who is struggling with _____. May they know they are not alone because I will be with them and so will our God. Lord, give comfort to those who have lost a loved one recently. May they know in their heart that the separation is only temporary. I pray the Holy Spirit will light my way to Your truth and make clear the simplicity of being one with God. Have Your way with me, Lord so that I am more compassionate, caring, forgiving, tolerant, accepting and loving. Jesus loves me this I know! Amen

When the Holy Spirit Calls
Luke 8:15

Oh, God, You are the giver of life. Thank You for also staying involved and part of my life as a guide, a support and an inspiration. You ask me to bear fruit- to be a branch of Your tree of life. Holy Spirit, when You speak to me, I need to stop and listen and then pay attention when a light goes on in an 'aha' moment. I know You give me messages, motivation and inspiration through scripture, books, sermons, music, friends and especially quiet moments. Guide me and urge me to pay attention to my intuition to be somewhere or to call someone. When You call me to do something, I pray I will take the time to do it. I pray I will expand my comfort zone to serve You. I am sorry for all the missed opportunities. Lord, lift me up and help me to lift others up with a smile, a helping hand or a listening ear. They will know I'm a Christian by my love and caring. I don't need to shout, preach or lecture. Guide me to build bridges instead of walls. In the name of Jesus, Your will be done with me and in all things. Amen

Walk With Me
Philippians 4:7-8 Ephesians 1:17-18

Thanks God, for creating me, loving me and saving me. Saving me not just for a fantastic forever life but also saving me every day from dangerous pitfalls in and out of my control. Often I am not even aware of the times You shield my body and soul from harm In this journey called life, I am so grateful that You are walking with me. Sometimes when I have a choice of going left or right, I choose the wrong turn. Sometimes I even know I'm on the wrong path but linger on it anyway. Lord, Your unconditional love walks beside me no matter what paths or turns I take so help me to learn from the choices I make. Holy Spirit, I will listen more intently on the path of good-ness and kindness as a seeker of Your truth. In name of Jesus Christ, prepare me for life's challenges and to be servant of Your will. Amen

Walk in the Spirit
Galatians 5:16-25

God of love, prepare me to walk in the spirit. I want my life to be a journey of continually growing to a greater spiritual maturity. Instead of being in conflict with myself, others and my community, I want to aspire to be more caring, more positive, more loving, more patient, more tolerant, more kind, more generous, more gentle, more fun loving and all around more in tune to the spirit of Jesus Christ. Father, I thank You for loving me. Thank You Holy Spirit for guiding me to find the way to the heart of Jesus. In the name of Jesus, I pray I walk with Your will on my mind. Amen

I'm Still Seeking
I Corinthians 13:11-12

God is good! God, You are so good that it is hard to imagine the scope of Your love and truth. I am so grateful that even in my spiritual infancy, I have a glimpse of who You are. I am still seeking Your purpose for my life and the true reality of my existence. As a child of faith, I need rules, guidelines, guilt and even some of the tassels and ribbons of liturgical worship to build my faith. As my faith matures, I pray the Holy Spirit leads me to a deeper relationship with You that is not as dependent on the need to perform in the right way, worship in the most theologically correct church or to donate financially. As I know You more intimately, my focus is to become a more loving person who is confident striding in the light of Your goodness. I am beginning to understand that mature faith comes from inside my soul. As this is happening, I don't need guilt or shame to live a good life. Instead, I am more motivated by Your love and love within my own soul to share my life with You and others in loving ways. Oh, God, thank You for being in my life. I want to continue maturing in my faith so I know, more completely, Your grand design. Love You!

Prayer for Purpose
Galatians 5:25

I am so thankful, Holy Spirit, that You dwell among us to guide (not enforce) us to grow in truth and knowledge so that we can know our purpose and put our purpose into action. We don't have to be smart to know Your will. We just need to be open to Your loving ways for what You ask of us is not a burden. Sometimes we are chained to our own choices such as addictions, isolation, anger, intolerance, apathy and resentments. Lord, help me to break whatever bonds that are choking my own freedom to soar with You and enjoy this wonderful gift of life. God is good. Guide me to Your truth. Amen

I Will Overcome
Matthew 11: 28-29

Selah means to pause and think
God of the Universe and of my family- thank You for today. *Selah*
Lord, help me to overcome the Goliaths in my life. The bigger than life issues that prevent me from being the best that I can be. With Your help and the support of others, I can overcome issues that distance me from You and the people in my life. I don't want to withdraw or struggle alone. God give me the strength to face my Goliaths face on. *Selah*

With the help of the Holy Spirit, I want to pursue the "good life" of being positive at home, work or school and to be helpful to others. Give me the motivation and courage to welcome someone new in my life to share my time and my faith with. God is in me and I am in Him. *Selah*

As God blesses me financially, I will be a blessing to others in need. I am thankful for the available opportunities to be of service to others in the community. *Selah*

Lord, I lift up _____ who has issues with_____. God, I am so glad I know you! Amen

God Loves- Do I?

Dear God, thank You for being in my life and a part of my life. I still have so much to learn about You and my purpose in this life before going on the next.

God loves the poor. Do I?
God loves people with lots of tattoos. Do I?
God loves angry teens. Do I?
God loves people born with deformities. Do I?
God loves people challenged with mental illness. Do I?
God loves people on welfare. Do I judge them without knowing their circumstances?
God loves prison inmates who are there for myriads of reasons. Do I?
God loves gays. Do I?
God loves people who practice their faith in other denominations and religions. Do I?
God loves people with dementia. Do I?
God loves people who sing loudly off key. Do I?
God loves me. Do I?

Small Things Make a Difference
Mark 3:31-35

Glory Halleluiah! What a great day to praise the Lord. When the sun shines, it lightens up whatever load we are carrying. I will take the time today to look at and appreciate the beauty of Your creation. Lord, help me to do small things with great love. Mother Teresa said it well.

Do Small Things with Great Love
We must not drift away from humble works because these are the
works nobody will do.
It is never too small
We are so small and look at things in a small way But God being
Almighty sees everything great.

Therefore, even if you write a letter for a blind man
or just go and listen, or take a meal to him, or visit someone
or bring a flower for somebody...
Small things...
Or wash clothes for somebody, or clean their house, very humble
work, this is where you and I must be. For there are many people
who can do big things, but there are very few people who will do
the small things.
Mother Teresa

When we do the small things for our planet like picking up litter or planting a flower in a bare spot we are doing Your will. When we read a book to a child, we are doing Your will. When we smile at someone in a waiting room, we are doing Your will. When we forgive thoughtless words,we are doing Your will. In all situations, I pray that Your will is done. Amen

Whatever I Have or Have Not
Ephesians 4:1-6

This prayer is inspired by the song, Whatever I Have, by Ken Medema
If used in a worship setting the music can be sung as a solo or a
group of choir members
Music: verse 1

You are my god and I am Your child. I am so thankful that I have the opportunity to grow in Your love and grace. I know that bad things happen to good people and that things will not always go the way I plan or want them to. I pray that when I am going through difficult times, I will not withdraw from You, my god. Instead, I will turn to You. No matter what my circumstances- my health happens to be...I can make it through anything as long as I am with the one who makes me who I am.

Music; Refrain then verse 2

You are my god, and I am Your child. I pray that I will never feel that I don't need You. Keep me from temptation and maintain greed at bay. I know You want me to be a success- but not at the price of ignoring my soul. Not at the price of thinking I am better than someone else. I pray that whatever I have, or have not, or who I am or am not; my faith in You, Lord, will continue to grow.

Music: Refrain then verse 3

You are my god and I am your child. There are times when I feel so alone- sometimes in a crowd, in times of grief, in fear of the unknown or in new surroundings like a different school, job or neighborhood. I may be alone standing up for what I believe. Always, Lord, let my voice be raised in clarity to praise, thank and love You.

Music; Refrain

I pray for clergy as they respond to their call to serve You. I pray for Your children in the military who may feel alone so far from home and family.

I pray for those with special needs of health, mind and soul- especially for_____.

In all things, Your will be done. Amen

A Whale of a Tale

Jonah said "no" to God because he did not want to go to Nineveh. Why?

Did Jonah not want to go outside his comfort zone for some reason?

Was Jonah prejudiced against the Ninevites?

Did he think the town was not worth his time?

Did Jonah think the Ninevites were a lost cause?

Did Jonah have more important things to do?

Did Jonah want to be in control of his agenda?

Did Jonah think he was not good enough to do what God was asking him to do?

Was Jonah afraid of failure?

Was Jonah overwhelmed?

How many times have I said "No" to God? How many whales will it take for me to say "Yes" to God? We all have feelings that tug at us to do something. Perhaps the Holy Spirit is nudging me to make a difference in someone's life or to right a wrong or to stand up for a cause or to become involved. Some common reasons people excuse themselves include being too young, too old, too poor, too busy, not smart enough, it is the wrong time, it is inconvenient, it is too risky, it is 'not my thing', not worth my time or whatever. How many whales will it take for me to say "Yes"? Make a fist. Inside your fist imagine the real and lame reasons for not saying YES to God. What do you want to hold on to and not let go of? Now open your hand with your palm up and blow those excuses away- Poof! Enjoy the sense of freedom. You are free to be the best you can be.

I am thankful for people who say "yes" when the Holy Spirit calls. I need to listen and take seriously God's plan for me. I have a purpose. Whatever plans You have for me, I know I will not be alone. If I am willing to let God change me and use my God given talents, my life will be rich with rewarding experiences. What I fear could turn to joy. Lord, I want to say "yes". Help me to overcome whatever blocks my progress.

In the name of Jesus, open my heart to do Your will. Amen

Fill Up With God
I John 4:7

Dear God, I am so in awe of Your greatness and goodness. Thank You for Your generosity that allows me to be alive and live in Your presence. With Jesus there is always Hope, Strength and Courage to go on regardless of my circumstances. Thank You for my friends who encourage, help and support me. Please bless their lives. Jesus, You didn't die so I can have a religion and go to church on Sunday. You suffered till death so I can have a relationship with You- a relationship for all eternity. Holy Spirit, fill my mind and soul full of God. Lift my spiritual essence to a higher level in communion with You. I pray Your will be done on earth and within me. Amen

CHAPEL PRAYERS

I wrote the following prayers to be used in our chapel. They were typed in the landscape format to fit onto a bookmark and printed on cardstock together. The prayers were then cut to be bookmarks.

Pray for Witness

Lord, help me to be more comfortable expressing my faith in You with others. I want to be a witness to Your love, forgiveness and salvation. I don't want to be embarrassed or shy – but I am. Holy Spirit, help me to know when and how to be a disciple of Jesus to my family, neighbors and all those I meet on my life journey.

Holy Spirit, inspire, motivate and guide God's children to share His story, plant seeds of faith, to live in His love and transform the lives of...

~The Prodigal Children
~The Lonely
~The Seekers
~The Agnostics
~The Grieving
~The Unchurched
~The Unaware

~_____

Matthew 9:37-38

Pray for Compassion

Lord, I pray that my faith matures to have compassion–not judgment for others.

I want to pray for the lost and disenfranchised without feeling self righteous. Holy Spirit, help me to understand that a lost soul is worth shedding tears about..

Inspire a desire within me to reach out to build bridges of friendship, trust and caring. I pray for the power of the Holy Spirit to move among us and shower both the churched and unchurched with the meaning of salvation and the curiosity to learn more. I pray that *name of church* continues to be true to our vision of being a welcoming place to worship.

Romans 10:1

Prayer for Boldness

Lord, help me to continually seek to enlarge Your kingdom by sharing Your story, living Your love and helping You transform lives.

Lord, help me to just walk across a room:
To say hello
To share a smile
To offer a prayer
To cook a meal
To advocate for fairness
To write a note or send a card
To take a risk To invite someone to _name of your church_
To share the story of the Resurrection
To sing a song
II Timothy 1:7-8

I Pray for Needs

Sometimes I need to witness to myself and walk across the room with God. My walk of faith is a journey that needs the sustenance of the Holy Spirit.

"Unto You, O Lord, I lift up my soul. Psalm 25:1
I need to thank God for the gifts that He showers on me every day.
I need to immerse myself in Scripture.
I need to admit my mistakes and wrong decisions.
I need to be more forgiving of others and myself .
I need to take the time to listen to the Holy Spirit who guides and inspires me.
I need a closer relationship with God.
I know God loves me. I need to trust in Him.
I need...
Philippians 4:6

*PRAYERS WITH A FOCUS
ON MISSION AND MISSIONARIES*

Ordination Prayer

This prayer was originally written for the ordination of a pastor. It can be adapted in a worship service for an ordination or call to service for Missionaries, Church Council, Deaconess, Christian Education staff etc.

The word, 'Amen', means 'So Be It'. or "This is true" I will pause during the petitions of the Prayer and say, Amen. Please answer with your confirmation of Amen. If you believe it, say "AMEN like you mean it. Amen... Where there is a blank underline fill in the appropriate name.

Let us pray together for God's children; for the church community, for those who hurt and are in special need of the Gospel and for all of God's creation. We also pray for _____ who from this day forward, will also be called, Pastor or Rev. etc _____.

Lord hear our prayer as:
We pray for the holy catholic church that tells the story of God's love in a myriad of languages and sings from the soul to worship You, Lord. May the Holy Spirit guide the church to be true to Your word and to be diligent in service to those who struggle physically, emotionally and spiritually. May the church be righteous without being judgmental. **AMEN**................

Lord, we pray that the members of Christ's church serve You with love and compassion and that we all strive to lead our lives according to Your will and Your values. May we all be role models to those who seek. Most of all, let us not be apathetic to the truth of Your existence and Your continuing commitment to humanity. **AMEN**................

_____ has been called by You, Lord, to become a pastor-and _____has enthusiastically responded. Holy Spirit be _____'s mentor so he/she will serve You with diligence and perseverance as he/she glorifies Your name. May his/her trust always be with You, Lord as _____ ministers to difficult people and deals with church politics. Holy Spirit guide Pastor _____ to build up the faith of the church with joy and love. **AMEN**................

Holy Father, we are thankful for and pray for all pastors, deaconesses, diaconal ministers, associates in ministry and for our bishops, May their faith continue to mature as they support one another in the service of Christ. **AMEN**.................

We pray for _____church. May the members be open to the Word of God, support the ministry of Jesus, and may the members flourish in faith with the help and guidance of Pastor _____ and the Holy Spirit.

We pray for a legacy of peace and ecumenicity within the world church. United, we can spread the Good News of Christ and minister to the needs of mankind. **AMEN**.................

We pray world leaders strive for justice, peace and equality. We pray each individual has the freedom to live in dignity to be the best person they can be. **AMEN**.................

We pray in Jesus name that in all things God's will be done. **AMEN**

Sending Missionaries
Matthew 28: 19-20

God of goodness, forgiveness and truth. Today is a day of wonderful goodbyes, best wishes and departing prayers for members of Your Kingdom who have received an invitation to serve You and have RSVPd with a resounding YES. Lord, prepare (*names of those going on mission fields*) to serve You in such a special way in a country rich with beauty and magnificent creatures You created. Where there is extreme poverty and tremendous life challenges just to survive, the culture is full of color, passionate music and optimistic people. Lord prepare the Mission team both physically and spiritually for a journey that may be life changing. Their intent is a wonderful thing that warms the cockles of my heart. I imagine it does Yours too. I pray the team arrives home safely and that their cups of faith be ever so full. Lord, I can also serve You right here at home. Holy Spirit show me the way and may all that we do; we do in Jesus' name. I love You, Lord. I am in Your caring hands. Guide me to when and where I should be. In the name of Jesus, Your will be done with the mission of sharing the truth of Your love and in all things. Amen

DEPARTURE FOR MY MISSION ABROAD

God of beauty and light- I am awed by Your power and by Your ongoing caring for all creatures living within Your creation. Thank You, thank You, thank You, Lord for the privilege of serving You and the people I will meet in _____. I am honored and humbled that You called me to serve in such a special way in a country rich with scenic beauty, smiles and of loving You, Lord. Please prepare me spiritually for this journey. All that I will do; I will do in Your name. If there are times when I might be tired, sore or uncomfortable; help me to rise up and gird up the ole loins to join in on helping my fellow Christians. I will try to do it with a minimum of whining and an abundance of laughter.

I pray new faces will know Jesus and accept the truth of God's love. I pray that together, we will experience the spiritual joy of getting to know You better. Lord, I pray that the Holy Spirit be with my friends and family I am leaving behind as I prepare for my adventure in _____. Please keep them safe and grounded in Your love. I pray especially for _____. I pray for my church family. May their faith be touched by the Holy Spirit. Lord, I pray that we all return safely to the arms of our loved ones. Lord, I pray for each member of the Mission Team. May we all have moments when our spirits soar to mountain top experiences never to be forgotten. I love You, Lord. I am in Your hands. Guide me to when and where I should be. In all things, Your will be done. Your friend, _(Your name)_____, Amen

Returning Home from Mission

God of goodness and beauty, I feel like I know You better since I touched the ground in *place of mission* and met some of the people here who have touched my heart. I am not the same person who boarded a plane *date.* I feel somewhat like I am leaving a part of heaven behind to return home to my family. I am glad that my experience will always be with me just as I felt the presence of my family and friends here with me in _____. Lord, please do not let me forget the beautiful faith filled friends who are now part of my life's memories. God of love, I pray for Your children who pray to You in a different language. Someday, we will all speak the same language in a place that is even more beautiful than *place of mission* and more beautiful than *hometown*. I pray especially for my new friends- (You can include their names). I will continue to remember them in my prayers to You. Oh God, there is still so much more to be accomplished here. I pray for the ill and needy that we did not see. I pray for those we did see and touch. I pray for all those afflicted with disease. Holy Spirit, be with children struggling to survive because their parents are dying or dead. Without You and Your servants volunteering here, those children would have no hope. Now they do! Bless this place we are leaving as it grows an abundance of seeds planted for the future. All kinds of faith filled seeds. Lord, bless the land and the buildings as they are being erected. I pray that there be a minimum of delays and glitches in the building process. Let each nail hammered into the buildings be a testimony of Christ's love and forgiveness. I pray that this land will always be used for Your glory. Teaching children is such a great way to glorify You.

Lord, as I wave good bye to *village/town/people* there is a lump in my throat. Part of me is glad to be going home while part of me wants to stay here singing, dancing and praying with Your children who are my spiritual friends. I know it will not be all fun and smiles as there will be difficult times along with joy as they continue doing Your work. Lord, I know their faith commitment is strong enough to fortify bridges of relationships that already exist in Your name. Bless _____ in ways they did not even know existed. I am so thankful for the blessings I have received while here.

Family and friends get ready. Here we come!! In all places, God's will be done with joy,

Let Us All be Servants

**Prayer for those serving as ambassadors of my church
to those who are homebound or in assisted living.**
Matthew 7:7

Let us pray with joy and thanksgiving. God of mercy, patience, oh, so much patience and everlasting love; we gather today to honor You and to give our support and gratitude to those who heed Your mission call to serve members of (*name of church_*)_____ during difficult and challenging times. Holy Spirit, we pray that You be with Your Servants as they minister to the lonely, homebound and ill. May Your insights be heard and give comfort and hope as prayers are lifted up and Communion is served to Christians who are not able to attend worship services.. Help them and us to feel the oneness with You, Lord, as we eat the bread and drink the wine in remembrance of You, Lord, I pray we understand that worshipping is just the beginning. Nudge us to use our gifts and talents to serve others. Lord, You are the greatest of role models. You ask that we also serve. We pray that we gain confidence to overcome our fears of serving in areas that seem uncomfortable to us. In Matthew 7:7 You tell us to Ask, Seek and Knock. Knocking is doing and sharing the joy of my faith with others. I pray that *name of church* answers the needs of those in distress. Let us then spring into action by knocking down the barriers that block our purpose of serving where You lead me to fulfill a need. Let us each pray for a moment to dedicate ourselves to service. (Pause for individual prayers) In all things, may we listen to Your word and heed Your advice to us. Amen! We ask that You lead our journey to the service where You know we can fulfill a need. Help us to seek a way to answer the needs of those in distress. Let us then spring into action by knocking down the barriers that block our purpose of serving where You lead me to fulfill a need. Let us each pray for a moment to dedicate ourselves to service. (Pause for individual prayers) In all things, may we listen to Your word and heed Your advice to us. Amen!

PRAYERS OF THANKSGIVING

Thanksgiving
Psalm 34: 8-9

This is a prayer guide. Where there is a ___, continue in your own words)

My Lord, You are so giving. If I were to start thanking You now for each gift that You have bestowed on me; I would still be here a month from Tuesday. Lord, I thank You for my family because_____. God, please bless them. I thank You for the mentors in my life who have shared their time, talents, friendship and faith with me._____.
I thank You, Lord, for music and lyrics that inspire me and lifts my spirit another notch. _____ . God, please bless all the musicians who make positive joyful noise. God, please bless them. Jesus, You told Pilot that Your kingdom was not of this world. I am thankful that I am on a journey to this world of Yours. _____ God, please bless my journey to Your kingdom. Everyone who pauses to listen to Your voice hears the truth of Your love. Our journey has bumps, crevices, smooth and rugged paths along with mountain top experiences. Bad things happen to good people and good people make poor decisions. I thank You for all the experiences of my life lessons. I pray the difficult times as well as my successes bring me closer to You. _____. Thank you for the abundance of blessings in my life including those that I take for granted every day. God, please comfort those who are hurting in some way. Thank You for loving me. I love You too. Amen

Prayer for Abundance and Clarity
Psalm 115: 14-15

Lord, I am so blessed to know You. It is my goal to have the veils of misconception flutter away as moments of clarity mirror the real You. Thank You for all that I have. Even in the leanest of times, there is food on the table and a place to call home. There is always enough to share at least a little. I am also thankful in times of abundance. It is Your will that I prosper. I pray that my family and I continue to increase our finances and that we manage all of our resources responsibly. Holy Spirit, thank You for giving me food and drink for my soul. I am blessed by God's grace. The great thing about spiritual prosperity is that it multiplies as we share our blessings. May Your will be done with me as I see Your image more clearly. Amen

The Turkey is Gobbled Up
Luke 17: 12-19

Father of everyone and creator of everything. The turkeys have been gobbled up (pun intended) and families have returned to their own abode after extended family and friends shared the traditional feast of Thanksgiving. The time of giving thanks, however, never grows old. I want to be like the 10th leper who after showing himself to the priests, came back to Jesus with a grateful heart full of thanks. When I give thanks, I am building on my relationship with You. Thank You God, for my life, my family and for the opportunities that come my way. Thanks for being my Lord and Savior. Thank You for the many miracles in my life. I am thankful for the pioneers who celebrated the harvests of their hard labor. I also appreciate the rich history of the original natives of America. Lord, each day prepare my soul to love You with a repentant heart and a resolve to make positive changes in my life. I will not forget how awesome my God is. Love You! AMEN

Laugh With Me God
John 6:35

God of our fathers and God of our Children. I come to You in joy, laughter and praise. You gave humanity a sense of humor so You must have one too. Help me to not take myself too seriously at times and to laugh at myself and to laugh with You. Thank You for all the beautiful sounds in our world. A Cardinal's quirky chirp- a child's giggle- Bach on a pipe organ- the rustle of leaves on a gusty day- the lapping of waves- the purr of a cat and a puppy's growl- a church choir filled with Your spirit and a pastor preaching when he/she is on a roll. These are a few of the beautiful noises that enrich my soul. God of all understanding, help me to see the big picture when things don't go the way I want them to. I trust in You that there is always light within the darkness if we don't turn our back on You. Help me to conquer the demons in my life and also the dark places within those who struggle with addictions, loose tongues, strained relationships, pain and grief. Keep me safe from times of trial. Thank You Lord for the bountiful gifts You give each day. I take so many for granted. I hope that You are smiling as I pray in the name of Jesus, that Your will be done in *(your city)* as it is done in Heaven Amen

The Joy of Loving You
Revelation 4: 8 & 11

Glory to God. I know that my Redeemer lives. Because of Your forever love, we also live now and forever. Thank You so much. In my life, I want to lift Your cross on high so others can see the joy of loving You. Because of who You are and what You do, Lord, Your name is sacred. Let me think twice before saying Your holy name in a flip or disrespectful way. Thank You, God, for all the miracles in my life. When I look at trees adorned with foliage that outdoes designers of the highest fashion, I am thankful for the magnificence of Your creation. Thank You! Thank You for my family and all those who have supported me, shared memories with me and love me for who I am. Thank you for my loved ones who have taken the journey to be with You. I look forward to seeing them and You in the future. I pray for someone I know who needs You. In the name of Jesus, Your will be done in the world and within me. I pray today for peace that transcends all understanding to my family and friends. Amen

Eye of the Needle
Matthew 19:24

Lord, I am thankful for all that I have. I am even more thankful that I know You and that You are in my life. Lord, sometimes I forget that being rich is relative. By global standards, I am very rich. I have more conveniences and have acquired more 'belongings' than the rich in Matthew's time. Sometimes I take the wealth I have for granted while there are people living in my community who are hungry, chilled on winter days or too poor to see a doctor. It is not the riches that make it hard to thread a needle. I think You want me to be a success. Perhaps the rich (including me) sometimes don't see heaven because we are so busy gathering stuff; looking at stuff and taking care of stuff. Just maybe we are so actively pursuing more stuff that we don't see what is right in front of us and within us. The problem is looking the other way from You. It is not what I have but what I do that opens the door to understanding. The eye of the needle is the door to understanding Your way and Your truth. Materialism can obscure our vision so we bump into or go around the eye of the needle. Holy Spirit, thank You for the 'Aha' moments when I see the truth of God's love and purpose for me. I pray that there be less greed and more sharing. I will share my wealth and my time. Heaven is within my grasp. There is heaven here and now if I only reach out. I don't even need a boarding pass or luggage to travel there. Lord, guide me to see You in new and exciting ways. I love You. Amen

God is an Artist
Philippians 4:6-7 Psalm 103:5

Father, thank You for being the giver of innumerable gifts. I take so many of them for granted, however I just want to express today that I do appreciate living in a world that is like visiting an art gallery on a daily basis. If I take the time to look, I can view Your artistic creations everywhere. You created the pallet of colors we enjoy in the evening sky and on the blooms bursting from the earth on a summer's day. You sculpted form to all creatures including mankind and either allowed or directed evolution to take its course. I have to admit there are some bugs I don't appreciate, however, other people do and all things have a purpose in the grand scheme of this earth we occupy. God, I am grateful that You not only created the Universe, You made it marvelously beautiful. I will do my part to take care of the earth and all that lives on it. I pray corporations and nations step up to pre-serve precious landscapes, marine life and foliage in our forests and jungles. In the name of God, our creator, I pray for preservation and appreciation of all living species. Amen

Thanks Before a Meal

Thank You God for the food before us.
We are one with the nature that brought this food to us.
We are one with each other.
We are one in grace with God.
Glory be! Amen

Grace Before a Meal

John 6:35 *I am the bread of life.RSV*

For life and food,
For a Positive mood
For love and friends
For everything Your goodness sends
Almighty loving God we thank You
Amen

We Gather to Give Thanks
Jeremiah 7:1-11 Matthew 21:13

Lord, You are awesome. Because of You, I have so much to be thankful for every day of my life. On Thanksgiving, Americans gather in homes to share a family meal with gratitude for their many blessings. I am especially thankful for_____.

I pray for peace, tolerance and forgiveness as families gather around Thanksgiving tables. I pray for loved family members who will not be physically present at the dinner table to celebrate the harvest of our lives. I am grateful for the time we shared with them and somehow I know their spirit will be present with our family on Turkey Day. I pray for peace and the safe return of our military who are not sharing a turkey and potatoes with their families. Thank You Lord, for Your greatest blessing of all- Your love that gives hope and anticipation for many Thanksgivings to come. Amen

PRAYERS FOR CHALLENGING TIMES

I can Choose to Learn from Hard Times
Psalm 34

Praise to You my God. I feel my being radiate as I feel Your presence with and within me. You are my guide. When I seek You out, You deliver me from all my terrors and hang-ups. You set me free. That feeling fills my soul with a positive energy of wanting to share my life with a loving God. With You at my side, I have nothing to be afraid of or ashamed of. Thank You, God, for guardian angels who protect and mentor Your children as we seek truth and purpose. Teach me, Holy Spirit, to respect and love God more completely. Teach me kindness and help me to control my tongue and to be honest in all that I say and do. Help me to seek goodness in others and strive for peace. Lord, I know You hear the calls of those in distress. Help me to hear Your call for me to help them. Lord, You are close to those who are broken hearted, depressed or in despair. I pray _____ allows the Holy Spirit to work Your wonders with their soul. Lord, help me to comprehend that bad things happen to good people as part of this life. It is not Your will, however, we can choose, with the help of the Holy Spirit, to learn and grow spiritually during and after hard times. Positive changes can occur from tragedy. The difficulties of this life are temporary as I pass through this life to another beginning of forever. I am sorry for my bad thoughts, words, actions and apathy. Thanks for loving me anyway and for Your unending forgiveness. Thank You for all the trees that You so beautifully created. As the leaves change hues during Autumn, I am astounded by the cycle of life they represent. The Fall of my life will also have its own beauty before I am transported to another world of Your creation. May I be open to Your will. Amen

Calming the Storms
John 6: 16-21

Jesus Christ, I don't need to be apprehensive of You because You are God. I don't need to cower before You because You have the power to calm violent seas. I need to respect You but not be afraid of You. When Your disciples met You on the stormy sea they were afraid because they did not know who You were when You called out to them. Knowing who You are is a lifetime quest and opportunity. I pray I take advantage of every opportunity to know You better. In this crazy world of shifting values and mixed messages, keep my heart from being hardened and cynical. I pray for help in calming the storms and dark places in my life. I do know that Your patience endures forever and that Your love has no boundaries. Thanks for being who You are and for loving me. May Your will be done with my life. Your loving child says, "Amen".

God Made Today
Galatians 3: 23-29 Psalm 8: 3-9

Selah means to think or ponder. After the word ,Selah, at the end of a paragraph, pause to think about what you just prayed and continue to talk to God in your own words.

God, You made today. So, today I will rejoice, enjoy and partici-pate. **Selah**

Lord, I am important to You. So I need to take care of myself not just for me and my family but also for You. Help me to make healthy choices in my life so that I will be even more of a blessing to others. **Selah**

Laughter can be an instant vacation. I am thankful for those moments and enjoy sharing them with You, Lord. No one is respon-sible for my happiness but me, however, I appreciate and thank You for the many blessings I receive from God the Father, Son and **Holy Spirit. Selah**

It is good to know that I am much more than a person- more than muscle, bones and a brain. I am a child of God. There is freedom from irrelevant rules, there is a knowing of being loved and of being significant in the vastness of the universe. How awesome to be part of the universe along with the diversity of peoples from various cultures, life experiences and faith backgrounds. Any child of Yours should be loved by me. There is unity in our faith of a loving God. **Selah**

Lord, I know You care about those who are in dark places and need healing, solace, encouragement and caring. I pray that they will be comforted by people of faith and that they know You are with them all along the way. May the peace of Your comfort be with_____. Guide me to someone that I can help out of his/her dark place.

Father, Son and Holy Spirit- the awesome threesome. Your love is so complete, so awesome it is hard to imagine. Nevertheless, You are real.

When I need to feel closer to You, I need to slow down, take a deep breath and experience Psalm 46:10

Be still and know that I am God.

Be still and know that I am

Be still.

Be **Selah** Ah yes, You are the way out of the darkness.

The Big "C" Touches Everyone

God of the universe, You are the creator of all things microscopic in size and more immense than all the planets in our galaxy. Some of the scariest and most dangerous hooligans are smaller than a grain of sand. Very scary real monsters are cancer cells that can invade any part of the human body. Everyone is touched by cancer either as a patient, as a family member, or as a dear friend of someone who is struggling with that dreaded diagnosis. I am thankful earlier diagnostic advances are saving lives. I am thankful for new treatment technologies that are increasing the number of survivors. Lord, ___ needs Your touch of hope and compassion to cope in the days and months to come. Lord, give me the words to encourage and to be with _____at the right time to help him/her during an especially difficult or painful moment. Lord, You know all about suffering and You are a survivor. It is OK to be afraid and angry, however, sometimes we can get stuck in a rut of negativity that impedes the emotional and physical healing progress. We need Your help, to work through those emotions so that they can be transformed to a positive healing energy. Lord, there is always hope. Help me and _____to think positive thoughts and remember how much we are loved. In the name of Jesus, I pray for healing, remissions and cures Amen.

Psalm 23

Lord, thank You for not giving up or getting bored with mankind after creating us. Thank You for being a shepherd who cares and will always nurture us even though some of mankind's actions give You reason not to do so. Thank You for providing us with our basic needs and the means to get so much more. Help me to know the difference between what I want and what is best for me in order for me to be the best that I can be. Guide Your children as we set our priorities and choose whom we will follow. Will I follow You, my Shepherd, or will I follow wolves? You want me to be successful and You want me to be accepted when I gather with family and friends. You also want me to spend peaceful time alone with You. It is then that my soul drinks in the knowledge of who You are. The solitary time restores me in an everlasting bond of Your love. A cup of love that spills over to touch and inspire others. If I live my life, in the name of God, I will make more correct decisions in my life and my values will reflect those of the commandments You gave to the children of Israel. Above all, to love one another. When I am faced with death or near death of a loved one or as I become closer to the end of my own journey I don't have to be afraid of anything. Not terminal illness, not sudden death, not terrorism and not self-doubt or guilt. I don't have to feel isolated, depressed or fearful because You are always with me. Your guidance, Your forgiveness, Your love and comfort lift me up. Lord, I have so much to be thankful for in this life and on into the next. Lord, the better I know You, the more fulfilled I become. The more fulfilled I become, the more I want to share and give to others while bitterness and resentments fade. It feels so good to be one with You. Lord, help me to see glimpses of the never-ending life I will have in the place You are preparing for me- A place of indescribable beauty that is all encompassing- A place of energy where everyone can be productive and useful- A place where I can feel great goodness about my transformed self as I stand in harmony with all the others. A place of knowledge, understanding, acceptance, peace and love. Thanks to You, I will dwell in such a place forever. Love You forever, Amen

Green Meadows and Shadowy Valleys
Psalm 23

Lord, You are my shepherd, my mentor, my confidant, my spiritual guide and my savior. I pray that as You lead me on my path in this life, I will hear Your messages and make the right choices. Thank You, Lord, for my home, family and all my belongings.. The more I follow the path that You guide me on, the less important my possessions become. I pray for those who, instead of Your values, choose self destructive lifestyles. Regardless of the chaos and trauma that may be surrounding me and my world, I know You are there to restore and heal my soul so that I can go on living with purpose. Lord, with You as my guide, I will cherish the values You have established. With Faith, Hope and Love, all things are possible. Lord, I know You are with me in the green meadows of success and the still waters of confidence. You are also beside me in the shadowy valleys of pain, fear, loneliness and death. Your love will comfort me during the difficult times in my life. I pray for my family and friends who need to feel the warmth of your touch. I pray especially for_____
_____. Lord, let my heart and soul be open to Your presence as I communicate with You in prayer today. The more I know You, the more joy comes into my life. I look forward to

living forever in Your presence in a place more beautiful beyond my dreams- A place of learning, beautiful music, laughter, stimulating conversation, friendship and all the good things that bring peace and harmony to life. May Your will be my will. AMEN

Evil Ways
Philippians 3:10

God is good. I am thankful that Your goodness- Your great and awesome goodness can overcome the evil in this world. It is often depressing to hear the daily news reporting the evil men do to each other. It is Your will to transform evil instead of always punishing cruel behavior. Turning evil around to goodness eliminates it. Revenge does not. Instead of pointing fingers at others, I need to face the darkness in myself. I must then admit it; reveal it and be aware of how my negative issues affect others. I confess that I am not without sin. Lord, I am sorry for the hurt I have caused others. Thank You, Jesus for understanding, transforming and forgiving! In the name of Jesus, I want my life to be according to the goodness of Your will. Amen

Plucking Petals Off a Daisy– is Divorce the Answer?

In the blank underline spaces insert the name of the person.

Father of all creation I am thankful for Your love.

God, I am confused and there are so many emotions flitting back and forth in my heart and brain. Do I listen to my heart or to my rational mind? I'm not even sure if my mind is rational. Is divorce the answer or should we continue to hang in there? I am exhausted with my thinking. Do I love _____? Do I love _____ not? Does _____ love me. Does _____ love me not? I am afraid of the consequences either way. Is guilt, anger, resentment, sadness or fear clouding my judgment.? Dear God, please help me work through my issues so that I will have more clarity while working on "our" issues. Can I forgive without allowing _____to continue hurting me or using me? I know that whatever happens within or without my marriage You will always be in my life. I have some difficult days and months ahead, however, I know my God will help me cope. I will get through dark days and in the end be a stronger person. Yes, with Your presence and help I will survive to become a stronger person. I pray for a friend, family member or counselor who will listen to me without being judgmental; who will not just tell me what I want to hear and will help me work out my plans for the future.

Whatever path my life takes, I know You will be walking with me. I know the Holy Spirit dwells within me to shed the light of understanding along the way. When I stumble as I know I will, my Lord will lift me up! I pray that both _____and I will follow in Your will. I want to maximize my full potential as a child of God. Amen to a spirit filled life.

Our Shepherd Watches Over
Lamentations 3:22-23 Revelation 7:16-17

Lord, I pray for healing, peace and knowledge of Your love to those who are ill, lonely or discouraged. Shepherd for all, please watch over and promote Your love and truth to_____. Holy Spirit, I pray _____ catches Your flame of Inspiration and of Knowing the divine essence of who he/she is. I love you, Lord. I am in Your caring hands. Guide me to when and where I should be in the name of Jesus. Your will be done with me in all things. Amen

Depression
John 1:5

Dear God. I know You are real, I really do. Sometimes I don't see the light of Your truth and love because I feel surrounded by darkness. Sometimes the darkness is so thick and heavy on my chest I struggle to lift my head up. I wonder if the light will totally blind me. I don't want to curl up and give in to the darkness again. Lord, help me. Your light shines on the inside of the darkness. The darkness will not prevail. It will not overcome me. I will say this over and over again. Your light will shine in my life. Holy Spirit, smile on me and give me clarity. I am loved and I will seek the light in my soul and my life. I will reach out to family, friends and caring professionals who will help build me up with positive nonjudgmental insights and encouragement. In the name of Jesus, I pray for Your emotional and spiritual healing because I can't do it alone. Amen to finding light and hope in the darkness.

Positive Energy
Lamentations 3:22-23

Today is a glorious day because You, Lord are in my life. Rain or shine, humid or breezy, I am thankful for my life. There are not only grey skies and threatening weather— there are dark, dry emotional times that I think will never end–but they do end unless I choose to get stuck. Lord let the testimony of my life not be filled with moanies for things done to me by others or circumstances not in my control. When that happens, Lord, help me to get over it and get on with my life. When I am stressed with challenges and don't know where to turn- I need to remember that my God makes a way when there seems to be no way. I will put my trust in You. There are days that I feel joyful and energized and that all is well with my life. Thank You, God for the good times. I want to share my joy with You and let You know how grateful I am. Holy Spirit guide me to share my abundance with others in whatever way I am gifted to do so. We are in this life together. Your love is in me and part of my whole being in this life and the life I will transition to when I am ready. It is a wonderful thing to be a child of God. Amen

When Disaster Strikes
Peter 1: 3-5

Lord, I pray for all the families whose lives have been turned upside down because of the _____ disaster. Your powers are even greater than the winds of raging hurricanes and swirling tornados. Be with the survivors as they heal in the months ahead and pave the way for new doors to be opened for them. Thank You for the dedicated rescue workers and volunteers who give rays of hope to devastated lives. Be with them as they continue their work. I pray, Lord, that You also be with the families here who are grieving for the loss of a loved one, loss of health, employment, a relationship or a dream. Help us all to know that when tragedy hits- it is not Your will. Help us to know, however, that You are in the midst of chaos to give encouragement, support and a way to restore order. Thank you for this day, I will try to make the most of it. Amen

Death is a Journey
Psalm 116:12-19

Oh Lord, in my confusion, my soul praises You. Death can be a scary quandary. The closer I and my loved ones are to the transition of being in the earthly body to another form in another place, the more anxious I become. I know it should not be so because You are with me and within me for all eternity. As I lift up my whole essence to You, I remember Your promise of salvation. Holy Spirit, quiet my fear as I face death for myself or a loved one. Please cover me with the Peace of Your Understanding which is a truth above and beyond the intellect. It is a knowing in my core that death will be the joyride of my life and a transformation to a better me. Instead of ceasing to exist, I will be more energetic. I will finally be free of all my stress, anxiety and the hang-ups I've been struggling with. I also won't be bothered by the hang-ups and quirks of my family and friends that I look forward to joining. I want to feel Your presence. I know You are here now all around me and within me. Amen to the fact that like the charming caterpillar who is transformed into an absolutely awesome butterfly, I will be transformed in the cocoon of Your love forever. Thank You for listening. Now I will stop chatting and listen to You.

Funeral Prayer

Inspired by The Lutheran Book of Worship, I led this prayer at the funeral of a church member and also my sweet aunt to bless them on the journey of their life.

After "God of mercy, love and life". The congregation's response is, "Hear our prayer and guide our lives"

I prepare to pray with a deep breath of thanks to a loving god.
I am thankful that *first name* loved- that *first name* **still** loves. I am thankful that *full name* was loved–that he/she **is still** loved very much.

Almighty God, in holy baptism You committed Yourself to *full name* and to all of us. We are gathered together in the body of Christ to give her/him honor and reflect on the goodness of her/his life. Give to Your whole church in heaven and on earth Your light and Your peace. *God of mercy, love and life-*

Hear our prayer and guide our lives.
Jesus Christ died a physical death and was transformed. We too will rise transformed after a physical death in sin to share a life of harmony and fun with God and my ancestors. *God of mercy, love and life-*

Hear our prayer and guide our lives
To those who mourn, we pray for courage and faith with a sure

and certain hope in Your loving care. May those who grieve come to You as they weep in sorrow so that they have comfort and strength tomorrow and for the days ahead. *God of mercy, love and life-*

Hear our prayer and guide our lives.

As we journey in our own pilgrimage of faith, Holy Spirit show us the light of Your truth. As the world surrounding us groans in fear, pain, sin and loneliness let the Holy Spirit lead us to Your world of love and harmony. Your world is also here and now in all I see, feel and even within me. Holy Spirit, encourage me to share God's love. *God of mercy, love and life-*

Hear our prayer and guide our lives

Awesome God, help us in the midst of doubts, apathy and things we can't understand. I believe You are real. Help my unbelief and inspire me to trust in the communion of all saints; the great forgiveness of all hurts past, present and future; and the transforming resurrection to everlasting life. Yes, that's forever. *God of mercy, love and life-*

Hear our prayer and guide our lives

God of grace, thank You, thank You thank You! By His death, our Savior, Jesus Christ, destroyed the power of death. By His resurrection He opened the kingdom of eternal harmony to all believers. Because Jesus lived- Because Christ died for a moment and lives again today- so *first name* lives today and tomorrow and forever. WOW! Instead of fear, physical death is to be viewed as a blessing for all believers. Someday, I will also live and dance with *first name*. Neither death or events in the world are able to separate us from the love of Christ. *first name*, enjoy your fabulous journey to be with God while sharing it with *name/names of loved ones who* have died (or you can just say, family members & friends) *God of mercy, love and life.-*

Hear our prayer
Amen

Toward the End of Days

Ecclesiastes 12 is a metaphor of old age and how the body is not what it used to be.

Father, You travel with us all along our life's journey. Thank You for Your guidance as we mature into adulthood. I pray for Your elderly children who have traveled up and down many roads and who now struggle in their frail bodies and sluggish minds. Many Seniors are living with their adult children, assisted living or in a nursing home. I pray they be treated with loving kindness and respect. It is also a challenging time for families who are the caretakers of their elderly parents. Lord give caretakers strength and will to lovingly carry on. I lift up *name* and his/her family. May they be aware that this life is not the end of the road. The best is yet to come. Lord, guide me to assist and encourage *name* in whatever way is needed. Amen

Unconditional Love

Dear God, I am so amazed at Your profound ability to love so many beings and creatures on this earth and maybe even elsewhere in the universe. Thank You, God, for Your unconditional love. A love that transcends all bitterness, betrayals, disappointments, apathy, anger, revenge and rejection of Your truths and way of life. It is so hard to let go of some of my hurts. There is a prodigal person in my life that chooses to be hurtful and negative or is immersed in a self destructive lifestyle. Can I continue to love _____while not accepting what he/she thinks, says or does? Holy Spirit, help me to understand. Help me to love _____ without enabling or hurting me and others again and again. Sometimes I need to remember that although "tough love" is hard to do; it is love. Holy Spirit, help me to know when I need to let go and love from a distance. If there is a time to confront or reconnect with _____, I pray for Your guidance to know the receptive time to share encouraging words and to also guide my thoughts and inter-action with _____. Dear Lord, Your will be done with _____ and with me. I love You! Amen

Prodigal Child
Luke 15:11-32

Lord of goodness and strength, You give light where there is darkness. You know my heart is heavy with anxiety for_____ who has disengaged from family, old friends, responsibility and faith in You.. Lord give me the wisdom to know the difference between being supportive and enabling _____ to continue living a self destructive lifestyle. Holy Spirit, I pray that someone will be able to reach _____ to shed clarity on his/her issues. I pray that somehow _____ will be motivated to look outside of him/herself to see there is a more positive and purposeful way to live. Lord, I don't know what else to say. You know I care. I don't want to be dragged down myself but I feel so helpless. You give me comfort in a challenging relationship. I will not give up hope that someday Your light will outshine the darkness. Holy Spirit, I pray You fill the void in _____'s_ life and ignite Your flame of clarity and truth in his/her soul. In the name of Jesus, I pray for a miracle and that Your will be done in the life of _____. Amen

Where Are You God?
I Corinthians 13:12

God, where are You? I am so angry I can't find You in the darkness of being hurt and scared. It is really not Your fault for the mess I am in but I don't know who else to blame. I will apologize later when I can see some light glimmering in the darkness. Right now I just need to vent and I know You can take it without getting even. I can't feel Your love in me now but I know You understand my feelings of frustration. You know me better than I know myself. Lord, help my body, mind and spirit to heal. Let the tremors of anxiety become an insignificant memory instead of up front blinding my essence to a future filled with never-ending possibilities in this life and the next. Father, Jesus Christ and Holy Spirit I know You will stay with me even though I have been withdrawing from You. I'm not seeing You in the mirror so clearly now. I pray for the haze to evaporate. Your troubled child is kind of saying Amen but I will begin taking baby steps to walk out of the darkness toward the light of Your love.

Good Riddance

There are several options for the symbolism in this prayer which can be adapted according to the circumstances. We all have issues that retard our emotional and spiritual growth such as anger, bitterness, addictions, self destructive decision making, resentment, guilt, shame, holding a grudge, lack of self control or the need to be in control. What are your issues? Write them on a piece of paper or on toilet/facial tissue. Another option is to imagine the issues inside your clenched fist. Whether on paper or imaginary, feel the issues in your clenched fist. You have been holding onto them and refusing to let them go although the weight of them is heavily constricting and dulling your life.

Lord, You are my confessor. You know me and love me with all my imperfections. You forgive me before I forgive myself. I don't want to keep holding on to _____. Help me to let go so that I continue to grow in Your grace and love. I am saying so long- adios- and goodbye to the pollution I have been harboring in my soul for way too long. It is time to release this negative energy that has been a dark cloud hovering over my life.

At this time your options are to: Place your paper in a bonfire or a wastebasket as garbage. Tissue paper can be flushed. If issues are imagined to be imprisoned within a closed fist, open your fist and blow the issues away. Shake your hand to get rid of any residue.

Lord, I am free. My body feels lighter and my mind seems liberated. Holy Spirit, help me to see my purpose more clearly now that a heavy burden has been lifted. Holy Spirit help me to stay with a positive perspective as my soul continues to mature in the way of God. In the name of Jesus, I wants to be free to be the best that I can be as a child of God. Amen

PRAYERS ON FORGIVENESS

Second Chances and More
Luke 23:39-43 Matthew 9:9-13

Thank You God for loving me as I am. Father, You gave so many second chances to Your chosen people in the desert and even beyond after their access to the promised land. Instead of being grateful for their freedom the Israelites repeatedly whined about their circumstances. You patiently listened to their complaints and gave them another chance when they worshipped a manmade idol of gold. Your words in scripture are filled with examples of great forgiveness and second, third and more chances. Oh God, I think You may have lost count of the second chances You have given me. I want to give myself a second chance to change _____ in my life and attitude. There are times when I feel like the Prodigal Son returning home. I do not need to be afraid because You always welcome a repentant soul. I am not alone in my struggle to change. Even if others do not understand, I know You do. Thank You for being there when I stumble. Thank You for loving me with all my flaws. I am not a failure. I am a work in progress as I lean on You when I can't develop more positive strategies in my life on my own. Holy Spirit, I want to grow in more positive and productive ways. Please guide my thoughts and intentions with moments of clarity and purpose. Your love is awesome. Amen

Good Morning God
Psalm 25: 16-18 Isaiah 43:13

God of all creation- good morning. Chatting with You is a great way to start the day. I pray that I can let go of the stresses of my life when I spend time with You. Help me to take breaks from stress when I feel overwhelmed. Help me to take control of my life and not impose my control on others. You, Lord, are my guiding light in murky waters. Jesus, You are the great forgiver. Help me to also forgive others who have hurt me and to forgive myself for my foolish mistakes. Lord, help me to remember that some days in this life I am the pigeon and some days I am the statue. I'd rather be like the sun shining on both the pigeon and the statue. Holy Spirit, on this day, let the power of God flow through me. Cast away my hindrances so that I can serve Your purpose. Music and Your word inspire me to love You more. God, bless the animals in my life. They give so much acceptance without being judgmental. Thank You for keeping me and my family safe in a place we call home. Thank You for the trees and colorful flowers cascading from hanging baskets enhancing urban landscapes. They add a touch of nature to manmade architecture. The unique beauty of Your creation is amazing. I need to take more time to appreciate Your artwork which is everywhere. Love You, God. Amen

It is Not Always Easy to Forgive
Matthew 18:30

God, sometimes it is so hard to forgive. It sure isn't always easy- especially when someone hurts me when I am vulnerable and when I have given so much. It doesn't seem fair when_____ doesn't seem to care and is going his/her merry way. Lord, help me to get over my bitterness and calm the storm of my anger. It is more painful to me than to those that hurt me. Help me to let go and get on with the rest of my life with peace and acceptance in my soul. I know You forgive me. You have also forgiven an infinity of negativity and wrongs in this world. It is all personal to You. Thank you. God, if You can forgive me I can forgive_____. In the name of Jesus, Your will be done in my heart. Amen

PRAYERS ABOUT ANIMALS

A Feline Prayer

Contributed by Smokey Bones and Zoe Rose

Oh God, this prayer is fur You. While relaxing on my comfy cat tree I gaze outside the window at the shifting clouds and leaves fluttering in the trees. I feel a oneness with the splendor of Your outdoor creation. Hey, there goes a bird and oh oh oh a chipmunk just stared at me before scurrying away in the bushes. It is too bad I can't move the patio door open. I sure could use a miracle now. I would love to chase the chipmunk and then gift it to my beloved human who takes care of my basic needs and more. Thank You God, for bringing us together. I would not have survived the elements and predators if I had not been rescued. I think all creatures, including humans, need rescuing for one reason or another. Now God, I don't want You to tell my pet humans how much I need them. I want them to keep thinking I am totally independent. After all, I have a reputation to live up to. I am thankful, God, that my pet humans think I am adorable. It must be true then that I am adorable. Well, adorably naughty. I am loved even in my naughtiness. I am forgiven teeth marks on toilet paper and other important papers, overturned house plants and the tons of hairballs here, there and almost everywhere. I am sorry for the catty hisses to the other animals in the house and for chasing and pouncing on them in the middle of the night. Because I am a cat I can't stop doing those things, without God's help. I pray cats of all breeds accept each other. We need to paws before extending our claws. I pray all cats have a safe place to lick and groom; food to survive; a sprig of catnip and some toys for fun. Oh God, You are purrrfect!! A meowy Amen

Living in the Kingdom of Peace

Genesis 6:19 Isaiah 11:6-9

Greetings my God of peace and love. It gives me a lot of joy to know that You love animals. It was important to You that Noah saved animals from the flood- and not just the animals for Noah's family to depend on for survival. I don't know where heaven is or exactly what heaven is like. The book of Isaiah gives us a clue that it will be a peaceful place where animals will not only will be present in our future, they will play and cuddle together as vegetarians (and maybe even as vegans). The thought of lions resting with a lambs while munching on straw is a real smile maker. This also makes me wonder that humans will also not need or crave meat in the place You have prepared for Your children. You know, Lord, I think heaven is a place I should definitely look forward to traveling to. Although heaven is a peaceable kingdom, I think it will be filled with positive energy, beauty, learning and precious creatures that I can love. Love, yes, love will be the force guiding all our thoughts and actions. Thanks so much that animals are in our lives now. Well, God, I know some birds and bats are very thankful for mosquitoes but they are one species I could do without on a summer evening. Hmm, if those pesky bugs are in heaven at least they will also be vegetarian. Ha! Thanks that animals are in integral part of Your creation and that we can share our lives with them. Amen

A Canine Lord's Prayer

The Lord's Prayer in the New Standard Canine Edition which is also available in the Cavalier King Charles Edition.
Contributed by Romeo and Charlie Woods

Oh great creator of trees and fire hydrants. You arf in a forever land of toys to tug, Frisbees to catch and balls to retrieve. I will only woof and never ever growl in Your name. A wag of the tail to Your kingdom of streams, meadows and woods to sniff and explore. This will be a place where all the humans and animals will co-exist in harmony. I hope there will be more of that good stuff in this world. Oh God, I pray I never run out of dog food and some treats now and then (mostly now). You know how I love to eat. I am thankful for sharing my huge dog house with a loving family who think I am their best friend. I love them too. Sometimes I am so tempted to be naughty because it is such fun to chew on shoes, sneak food off the table and run around the house just for the fun of it without caring whether something topples and breaks. I am especially tempted when my human friends go somewhere in their big metal thing with rubber wheels without me. Sometimes they are gone for an eternity and I wonder if they will return. Oh, but I forgive them when they return. I get so excited to see them my tail wags uncontrollably. I pray that all dogs and some cats (only kidding, all cats) are treated kindly. I am so thankful for vets and rescue places that help animals. A woof of anticipation and a wag of my tail to a forever existence of unconditional love with lots of hugs and petting hands. May all animals and humans wag more and bark less. I will paws to think about this. Amen

Grieving the Loss of a Pet

Add your pet's name in the blank spaces.

Lord, first I want to thank You for the time I had to share my life with_____who brought so much joy and fun into my life. I miss, _____, who was also my friend, more than I realized I would.

I can't imagine a world without animals. In my heart, I do wish we will be reunited someday. Although some people may think me silly because I grieve for a pet; I know You understand. My grief does hurt and right now I feel empty because _____ was a large part of my life.

It is a relief that _____ is not in pain. I really am thankful for the time we had together. Animals are a most amazing part of Your creation and such a blessing to humanity. _____ taught me lessons on living, loving and forgiving. Thank You, Lord, for listening and understanding. I am grateful _____is at peace and that we shared a beautiful moment in time. Good journey, my friend, and go with God. Amen

PRAYERS ON UNITY

The Church United in God's Love
Ephesians 4: 11- 16

Jesus, You are the Savior of all. I pray for respect and understanding between people of various religions and among differing Christian denominations. We are all children of our creator father and we are all forgiven sinners because of Your sacrifice. May we be united in love for each other and cooperate with a mission of service doing Your will. Lord, we can build up our faith together. United in purpose we can not only accomplish a greater impact of service to our earth and humanity, we can learn Your truth of love from each other. United we grow as the Holy Spirit speaks the truth to our individual souls. God bless us all and Holy Spirit guide my journey of faith with truth and love. Amen

I Put My Trust in God
Psalms 37:3-5

Father, You are not God of Gods. You are the only God. It is only You that I can put my complete trust in. The more I trust You, the more I will follow Your guidance to a fulfilling life. Father, You give me so much and ask for so little. Thank You for the gift of today. I will open it with excitement. Lord, I decide to be happy and positive today. With Your help, I will accept change as an adventure. I will work on accepting the losses in my life as an education and disappointments as an opportunity to open new doors. Church bodies have been debating and struggling with various issues since the early church. Today many denominations and congregations struggle with accepting more 'modern/contempory' worship styles and individuals who aren't "traditional'. I pray issues such as body art, contemporary music, theological differences or accepting gay Christians does not divide any church. Help us to remember that we are all Your children and that it is not our place to judge. It is Yours. Help me to accept my fellow Christians even though I may disagree with some of their opinions or lifestyles. Lord, be with those who are living in a relationship where there is abuse and battering. Lead them to the help they need to survive. I pray for those who are in need of healing. Guide those who are researching for cures to find answers that will save Your children and their families the trauma of MS, cancer and other diseases. I pray for Your healing touch especially for_____. In Jesus name, enlighten my soul so that I may serve more abundantly. May Your will be done in the hearts of Your children. Amen

Let There Be Peace
Psalm 85: 8-13

Lord of Peace, You are the Peacemaker. You taught us how to embrace peaceful thoughts and actions. I pray for peace among nations. Let freedom take form and grow where it is stifled. I pray that world leaders stand up for peace and negotiation.. I pray that extremists with terror and hatred on their minds be converted to a new order of peace. May their anger be stilled with rationality and mutual acceptance of other cultures and religious beliefs. Lord, I pray that peace is a reality within me. Help me to be more accepting of all Your children. Holy Spirit, You came to inspire and teach people of all languages and backgrounds. I need to remember that Jesus came to save us all by His Grace. Peace to all. Amen

The Temple of God

May my place of worship always be a place where the priorities are prayer and worship so that the trappings are a means to grow in faith rather than the focus. In the words of Jeremiah, "This is the temple of the Lord". It is here where we learn to be tolerant of aliens, orphans and widows. What does that mean for me whenever I am sitting on a pew in (name of city)_____ ? We are to act justly with each other. How does that affect me? Who exactly is each other? Who are the aliens? Father, Son and Holy Spirit I am most thankful that You are a god of love, peace, justice and forgiveness. Thank You for the amazing grace we are all blessed with every day. In the name of Jesus,

I will share the love without being judgmental. Thanks for giving. I love You. Amen

Lord Expand My Outlook
Luke 6: 31

God, Your love is awesome. You have given so much and expect so little in return. I pray that the Holy Spirit helps me to stretch my outlook on the way I look at and treat others. Help me to be less judgmental—that's Your job anyway. Lord, help me to expand my area of comfortableness around others that I 'perceive' to be unsightly or different in appearance or lifestyle. Help me to be more accepting of others who convey a diverse political or religious philosophy. Holy Spirit, also motivate children to stand up for students others make fun of or bully. Lord, I pray for those who feel ostracized or isolated because of a physical handicap or mental challenge. May their sense of self worth give them strength to be the best they can be. Lord, I want to be Your servant to share a kind word and a smile every chance I get. Your will be done even in some of the seemingly insignificant things Amen.

THE LORD'S SUPPER

Christis the Bread

Christ is the bread, awaiting hunger St. Augustine

Lord, I want to think about Holy Communion. It is somewhat a mystery to me. I know it is an important part of my faith journey. Is the Eucharist not so much a religious doctrine to be labeled by various Christian denominations as is coming to the Holy Communion table a gift from Jesus to be experienced? Jesus invites us all to the table and those who RSVP have the opportunity to be one with Christ. Communion is not just for saints, it is also for sinners hungry for spiritual clarity and to fill an emptiness they don't understand. Jesus, You invite me to participate as we share a meal of bread and wine. I want to experience the spiritual closeness of being one with Christ. Lord, thank You for the many opportunities I have to experience Your love, compassion and grace at the Communion table. May each time enrich my soul and nurture my faith in the Son of God. In the name of Jesus, I pray for clarity of truth and a kind heart. Amen

Touching Base With You God

II Corinthians 1: 3-4

Lord, it is so good to touch base with You on this beautiful day. I am pausing to worship You and reflect on how wonderful it is that You are a large part of my life. I look forward to sharing the meal of Holy Communion whenever I have the opportunity. A meal that reminds me of Your sacrifice for my eternal life. Yep, that means we will be together forever. Lord, I believe in Your miracles- both seemingly insignificant and unbelievably wonderful. I believe You can heal mind, body and spirit. Thank you, Lord for all the miracles in my life! Even those I am not aware of. There is someone I know that needs Your healing touch… an experience of clarity… a peaceful moment… a job opportunity… a perception of Your truth and love.. I pray today especially for………………………… In all things, I pray in the name of Jesus that Your will be done. Amen

ADVENT–CHRISTMAS SEASON

Holiday Lights

Greetings God! Christmas lights are already displayed in stores although it is not even that close to Thanksgiving. A few eager beavers already have holiday lights casting colors on their houses and shrubs. The closer we get to Christmas, the more brilliantly creative the lights shine through the darkness of December nights. How fitting that we use lights to celebrate the light of the world. Thank You, Lord, for the opportunity of being able to worship You in a place of my choice and in a manner that inspires my faith. Thank You for beautifully harmonious music and the talented musicians who share their passion. Stirring music can bring my spirituality to a higher level. Lord, sometimes, my soul soars to lyrics proclaiming our love for each other. Holy Spirit, I pray for Your inspiration and guidance to show me clarity as I seek the truth of the oneness that I share with my triune god- Jehovah, Jesus Christ and Holy Spirit. I am one with God. Wow! I need to take a moment to let that sink in. Lord, You light up my life. Amen

Advent–I'm Waiting to Celebrate

I can come just as I am to pray and to attend Your Birthday party. Lord, I am waiting to celebrate Your birthday. My goal is to prepare for Your party by giving more of myself to You and others. I usually get carried away with decorating, shopping for gifts and going to and fro gathering with family and friends. I need to remember Christmas is all about You and the honor of Your visit to mankind. That was an incredible history making visit that makes all the difference in my life. Jesus, This Advent I will take time to be quiet in gratitude.

Lord, I am thankful for the children in my life who embrace Christmas with enthusiasm.

Lord, I am thankful for my church family who want to serve You during the Holidays.

Lord, I am thankful for beautiful Christmas music that brings me closer to Your presence.

Lord, I am thankful for new technology and medical advances that saves lives.

Lord be with our military as they serve America to preserve peace and freedom and who prepare for Your birthday while missing their home and family.

Today I lift up ___(names)___. May they know they are surrounded in Your love.

In the name of Jesus I pray for Your truth to be known among all mankind. Amen

Mary Says Yes to God's Gift
Luke 1:46-55

Advent ~ This is a time to celebrate and it is a time to prepare for celebrating Your Birthday. As I prepare for this Holy day, I pray the Holy Spirit reminds me that it is a time for giving rather than taking. I pray I do not become confused by the roaring waves of people in the mall, the stress of getting the gifts and decorating with pizzazz. Holy Spirit, remind me to add a prayerful touch of Jesus to each card, cookie, dinner and gift that I share with family and friends. Jesus~ You are the image of the Gift itself and how a Gift is given. Your mother, Mary embodies how the Gift is received. She is the perfect YES to God. Help me to receive the gift of Your love every day and to know deep in my core that You choose to love me. Lord, I pray for Peace.... Peace within myself....Peace in my family...Peace with neighbors and co-workers...Peace where there is bigotry....Peace in families where fear dominates...Peace to eliminate bullying...Peace where there is war. Where there is a void or emptiness in people's lives, I pray that they look to You. May they actually see who is already a presence in their lives and seek to find You within themselves. Children~ How You love them! I pray they know the real reason for the season is You. In the name of Jesus, I pray there will be good tidings of great joy in all the lands of the earth. Amen

Prepare Ye the Way of the Lord– Advent Prayer

Philippians 4:4-7 Luke 3: 7-16

If this prayer is used in a worship service, a vocalist can sing the phrase "Prepare ye the Way of the Lord" which is a song from the play, Godspell which is the inspiration for this prayer.

Prepare ye the way of the Lord Thank You, Father, for sending Your Son to live among us; to be one of us and for Jesus to understand what it is like to be human. Thank You, Jesus, for showing us how to love our God, who is in all of His creation. Thank You for saving us from ourselves and the forever shadows of evil.

Prepare ye the way of the Lord I pray that this year, I will focus more on the joy of Christmas than the duties of Christmas. Lord, be with me as I shop and or make gifts for the people in my life so that it be more of an adventure than a drag. I will also gift them with prayer along with the material gifts-

Prepare ye the way of the Lord I pray for families throughout the world who are hungry for enough food to survive today, who are thirsty for education or who are craving for freedom. I am thankful that there are opportunities for me to help- not just at Christmas time but throughout the year. Holy Spirit, I pray for people who feel lonely, depressed, isolated or are grieving. My Lord, who is gentle of heart, let them know that they are loved by You and that other people care about them. Holy Spirit, motivate and guide me to help.

Prepare ye the way of the Lord I rejoice that God is in me and that I have many opportunities to experience Your presence more intimately as I prepare for and partake of the Lord's Supper. I prepare for this communion with You by admitting my hang-ups and missed opportunities to serve. I'm sorry.

Prepare ye the way of the Lord Lord, I pray for Your comfort, healing and gentleness to surround....*name persons*........

Prepare ye the way of the Lord Lord, I pray this holiday season I will be more of a 'Soul' man or woman than a 'Material' girl or boy. Along with the shopping and wrapping, I will prepare for the celebration of my Lord's birthday with prayer, worship and medita-tion. I look forward to my arrival in Your kingdom of Peace, Beauty and Joy. Love You, Amen

Jesus Is The Reason For The Season
Luke 1: 30-35

God of love, I am visiting You with joy this Christmas season. The melodies of Christmas bring me closer to You. I pray that Your miraculous birth will overshadow the presents, food and Santa as Christians celebrate Your Birthday. We need to remember that it is about You—not about us because You are the reason for the holiday season. Lord, during the holiday season and throughout the year, guide me to scatter seeds of love and faith with smiles and enthu-siasm. Holy Spirit, may the lonely and depressed be lifted up; know they are loved and that they have a divine purpose to their lives. I pray for those who turn their back on Your divinity and Your grace. Holy Spirit, let Your enlightenment touch their souls with clarity of Your truth. I lift up people and families who are grieving as they miss sharing the Holidays with loved ones. May they be comforted in the knowledge of future gatherings and celebrations together. After all, that is why You were sent to earth. Your birth is our eventual re-birth to a glorious life forever encompassed in the open arms of Your love and those who are already there. I pray for holiday travelers. Keep them safe and sober. Glory Hallelujah. I will keep You in my mind as I prepare for the celebration of Your Birthday. During this Christmas season, God's will be done in the hearts of mankind. Amen

Oh My Santa

Lord, I've been wondering. If I cussed in the name of Santa; would I be flogged in a mall? Does good old St. Nick deserve more respect than You? Hmmmm... Are the gifts Santa allegedly puts under the tree greater gifts than those of the spirit? Thank You for all life, for all the things I take for granted and especially for Your love that is beyond my understanding. Santa is fictional. You are real. You are real to me. Love You, Lord! Amen

Glory Hallelujah- I Pray with Joy

Glory hallelujah! I pray with joy today. Glory hallelujah! I am so blessed. God, You loved humanity so much You sent Your beloved son to live among us. Thank You so much for that gift that just keeps giving, loving and forgiving. May my gifts to You and at least some of my gifts to others this Christmas season be more in tune to Your values than our cultural "Gotta Have It" materialism. I love the uplifting holiday music. Singing carols brings joy to my soul and a smile on my face. I look forward to celebrating Your birthday, Jesus. What will be my Birthday gift to You? *(Take a deep breath and pause to think about a birthday gift to Jesus.)* Glory Hallelujah! Amen

Drink in the Gift of God's Love
Luke 1:30-35

Jesus, You are the reason for this glorious season. I give homage to You as Christians around the world celebrate Your birth. I don't know what You think about the commercialism, bling and busyness we surround ourselves in that often causes more stress than inspiration. At this moment, I want to put that aside. I need to take a deep breath… and drink in the gift of Your love. Thank You for leaving paradise to enter the world of mankind so that You could understand us and so that we can better understand You. I have so much to learn. I pray that the Holy Spirit continues to guide my journey of faith. I pray for my family. I pray that, as a family, each year we will display more symbols of You and less of the secular. I pray that our thoughts and actions will be more reflective of the real reason for the season. The real reason for the season is to wish You a Happy Birthday and to reflect on the significance of the Son of God joining with mankind on earth. Happy Birthday, Jesus. Thank you for the joyful music of Christmas. Bless those that compose and render the beautiful notes of fanfare proclaiming my faith. Thank You for all the people who have planted the seeds of faith in my life and for the pastors and missionaries who share their lives and faith here and everywhere. Bless the children. I know they are special to You. Lord, be with our military and their families who are spending Christmas away from each other. I pray for all those who are lonely, grieving or depressed. May the Holy Spirit comfort and encourage them. Lord, I love you. In the name of Jesus, I pray for worldwide peace as Christians celebrate the gift of Your presence among us. Amen to the Alleluia chorus!

Where There Is Truth There Is Light
A post Christmas prayer
II Corinthians 4:6

This is a Selah prayer. After Selah, stop and think or continue chatting to God in your own thoughts and words. Begin by taking a deep slow breath through your nose thinking "Yah and exhale through your mouth thinking "weh". Now pray to Yahweh, your awesome god.

God, You are the light of the world. Your light shines on the truth as I try to find my way in the shadows of who I think You are and how I fit in the puzzle of living within Your creation. **Selah**

Am I trying to shape You, God, instead of allowing You to shape me? Whenever I follow Jesus, I will never walk alone in dark tunnels of misconceptions and when I accept Your truth, my soul is free to experience fantastic possibilities. **Selah**

We lit up our homes and towns celebrating Your birth with beautiful lights. Some of those lights are now unplugged resting in boxes. You, my Lord, never go unplugged or half lit. **Selah**

Jesus arrived as a completely vulnerable infant who reveals God as being perfectly and totally lovable. **Selah**

Thank You, Jesus, for being the light of my life as the reality of Your love and grace is opened more each day! I want to be a window of light that shines through for others to see Your love with an open door invitation for them to follow You. **Selah**

We are all united as one family with You as our Father. Direct me where I can be of help to families of the world who need comfort, peace and healing. **Selah**

I will walk in the light of God's grace forever. **Selah**

Take a deep breath in thinking "Thank"... Slowly exhale thinking "You" Amen

LENTEN AND EASTER SEASON

Ash Wednesday-
A Reminder of Transformations
Mark 9:2-8

Ash Wednesday is a reminder that life, as we know it, is fragile without the life and sacrifice of our Lord, Jesus Christ. As the Lenten Season dawns in another year, Christians remember the depth of God's love for us. It is a time to experience an array of feelings. Emotions of a swelling <u>grief</u> as Lent progresses toward Good Friday- <u>Guilt</u> that Jesus suffered and died for me. <u>Relief</u> that I am more than just dust returning someday to the earth- <u>Anticipation</u> of Easter's reunion with the blossoming rebirth of the fruit of the earth.

Holy Spirit, I pray that I continue to grow in understanding of Your Master Plan for me and all humanity. In a rational mind and with an open heart, I pray we all build on our relationship with You. Jesus, I believe You are the son of God who was transfigured before men and later died for my sins so that we can all transform with enlightened spirits. Jesus, Son of God, You gained and maintained Your inner strength to complete Your purpose of saving humanity by communing (praying) *with** Your father. Your task as a man of the world was to teach and to save. Lord, I want my faith to mature and grow. I want my inner strength to be strong as my prayer life progresses to higher levels of enlightenment. I pray I set the proper priorities to make it so. Jesus, I believe You are the son of God who died for my sins so that with the inspiration of the Holy Spirit we can all transform with enlightened spirits. Your love lasts forever. Amen

* I used 'with' instead 'to' because it wasn't just Jesus talking to his father. They had a two way communication.

Lenten Prayer of Thanks

Thank You, giver of life. I have so much to be grateful for. As I experience this Lenten season, help me to understand what You endured in order to give me and all of humanity the greatest gift of all. The gift of sharing life everlasting with You. Without You, Jesus, death would be the end–Period- kaput–extinct–Instead, I am now in the womb of everlasting life waiting to be reborn into a new life of amazing beauty and total love. Jesus, thank You for being baptized as a human person. A man that experienced temptation- not just in the wilderness but throughout Your humanity. You also experienced rejection, disappointment and both physical and emotional pain. You understand my difficult times because You experienced them 1000 fold. Lord, You have so much love that keeps giving and giving and giving. Thank You! I am sorry for taking You for granted and by sinning in so many ways. Yes, the Lenten Season can be a downer but it is the prelude to the greatest and most wonderfully joyous celebration. EASTER!!! I BELIEVE. I believe that this life is a preparation for the next. Be with me Lord as I prepare to meet You each and every day. You are a God send. Love You and amen.

Mixed Feelings

During this Lenten Season I have mixed feelings. Sometimes I feel like I have a low grade depression as I ponder the sacrifice You made for my sins. I guess I need to feel some of Your suffering so that I can understand and be grateful for the sacrifice You made. Thank You, Jesus, for becoming a man in order for me to become a free spirit. I have no need to fear death. Because of You, death makes sense. Lord, because of Your sacrifice and grace, I have hope for the Prodigal members of my family. I pray the Holy Spirit be with family and friends who distance themselves from family, friends and You. Jesus, You surrendered to excruciating pain, humiliation and death for all humanity. However, when I surrender my heart to God, I am filled with peace and joy. It is *a knowing* that God fills my spirit with abundance. I pray I continue to spiritually mature with the deepest trust in

You, God. I will spend more time alone with You so that I can be my most loving self as I explore Your spirit within me and listen to Holy Spirit touching my soul. Thank You God, for loving so much! Amen

The Power of God's Love
—Colossians 1:16-20

Lord, during this Lenten Season, I am more aware of the power of Your love. As we approach the anniversary of Your death, I am both sad and grateful. I am sad that the sins of mankind are so horrible that Your sacrifice was necessary. I am sad that what You went through was so physically and emotionally painful. I am so grateful that You had the courage, strength and awesome love to go through with it. I don't even want to think about what the alternative would have been. Lord, I and all humanity do not deserve such a sacrifice- but You did it anyway. Our sins are forgiven. Yay! I pray I will also be able to forgive those who may not deserve it. Help me to know that I can forgive someone without enabling them to continue hurting themselves and someone else. Holy Spirit, move among us in all corners of the world and inspire us to walk tall and boldly as we share Your Word with the message of a true God, who loves, forgives and breathes eternal life into our souls. I am grateful, God, that You want to have a relationship with me and want to share beautiful moments with me. You are waiting for me, like the thief on the cross, to join You in a place that is beautiful beyond comprehension. I pray for those who need Your healing touch. I pray for those who can't see Your light because of addiction, depression, anxiety, guilt, grief or apathy. Help them to see more clearly and to know there is hope in this life and the next. I pray especially for _____who is close to my heart. Thank You for the comfort that You give them. In all things, Your will be done and that doing Your will always be a priority in my life. Amen

Palm Sunday–A Bittersweet Day

John 12: 12-19 Philippians 2:5-11

Lord, today I celebrate what must have been a bittersweet day for You. Everybody loves a parade and You were not only the Grand Marshall of the parade, You were the main attraction. It must have felt good that so many people appreciated who they thought You were and You did have Your adoring fans.

God, the Trinity, You really want a relationship with each and every one of us. In His humility, Jesus does not ask for our worship. Christians don't have to be festively waving palms while shouting Hosanna to Jesus, our Savior, while celebrating Palm Sunday....and yet, Jesus, I want to express with joy the love filling my heart for You. Thank You, Jesus, for taking the tough road that followed the parade. As You were riding along and watching the sea of waving palms, You knew what was ahead for You in the following days. Cheers of joy turned to tears of grief for Your disciples and family. Lord, prepare my soul as Christians throughout the world pass through another year of remembrance during Holy Week. I will take time during this holy week for moments of stillness so that I can feel Your presence and the significance of Your sacrifice. Jesus, Your divine nature came to us not as a monarch but rather as a servant. Jesus, You are Lord of my heart and I pray that with the help of the Holy Spirit, I too will become a servant. Holy Spirit bend my thoughts to seeking the truth of Your humility and compassion. There is joy in knowing and doing Your will. I pray the footsteps of Missionaries, Sunday School Teachers and Youth Leaders tread with the charisma of the Holy Spirit as they assure a new generation of the joy of being in a relationship with our God. In a changing society, youth need You more than ever as enticing temptations to seduce teens can lure them from the paths of Your harmony and everlasting love. Lord, the military and their families are always in my thoughts as I know they are in Yours. I pray for their safety and speedy return to the ones they love at home. Let there be peace in the Holy Land this week. Thank You, Lord for the many blessings in my life as I lift up _____ for Your healing comfort. God of love, I wave my palms in honor of You today. Holy Spirit, prepare my heart with prayer and service for the way of

You, Lord so that I continue to strengthen my relationship with You. With a wave and a joyful shout, Amen!

Maundy Thursday–
Blessed be God Who Forgives
Matthew 26: 36-46

Lord, I prepare to remember Your darkest hours. Although it is sad and it is scary- it is a story of ultimate sacrifice and love. *Blessed be God who forgives.*

Christians point our fingers at Judas. Can I count the times I have betrayed You, Lord, by my actions, words and sometimes silence? I am sorry for the times I have turned my back on You or called out Your name with disrespect. *Blessed be God who forgives.*

Christians don't understand how Peter could deny You 3 times. Can I count the times I have been too embarrassed to mention Your name or stand up for You? This year, I will walk across more rooms to build friendships in Your name. *Blessed be God who forgives.*

Lord, my heart is heavy with sorrow for all the pain, isolation and humiliation that You experienced to save mankind from a destiny of a completely final death. You love us so much that You want to spend eternity with us. Because of You, death is just the beginning of a transformed life filled with a beautifully productive, meaningful and purposeful eternity. *Blessed be God who forgives.*

Thank You, sweet Lord, for Your sacrifice and forgiveness. B*lessed be God who forgives.*

Maundy Thursday–
The Passion of Your Love

My dear Lord, my heart is heavy and I am depressed as I think about the pain and torture You sacrificed for mankind- for me. Our souls are as dirty as the feet You washed so long ago. Although no one deserves Your grace, redemption and love; I thank You, God, for those great gifts. Even though Your trial of pain and sorrow happened centuries ago, I need to feel a touch of the whip and the piercing hardness of nails in order to understand how much You love me. You deserve the utmost respect! A tear in Your honor this week will make Easter more joyful and meaningful. I pray the Holy Spirit will touch lives around the world this evening and throughout the year. Holy Spirit, move our hearts to be disciples of Jesus wherever we are and however we are gifted to do so. I pray for all those who lead us to a better understanding of the big picture of Your love and the future we will someday spend with You. For that is what Maundy Thursday and Holy Week are all about- The Passion–The Passion of Your love. A love so great that You would endure anything to keep us with You forever. I love You too! Amen

Good Friday–The Ultimate Sacrifice of Father and Son
Mark 15:37-39

Lord, today Christians around the world are observing the anniversary of Your love on the cross. My Father in heaven sacrificed His son. How painful it must have been for God, the Father, to be there- to see His Son in His final hour of sacrifice- and then to look away for a moment. Abba, did you look away in order for the sacrifice be totally absolute -or was it because it was too painful for a Father to watch? God, the Father and God, the Son loved and continues to love mankind so much that they both made the ultimate sacrifice. Holy Spirit, help me to be there as I remember the events and the people of so long ago. As I relive the Passion; I want to know in my soul how great Your passion is for us. When storms of doubt, grief and disappointments in life, seem to engulf me, I need to turn to Your open arms of comfort, understanding and peace. Lord, I pray for those who need Your comfort and forgiveness- for those who come to You in prayer and also for those who don't ask for Your help. My thoughts are also with the men and women in the military who also know the meaning of "sacrifice'. I am looking forward to celebrating Your resurrection on Sunday. In the name of Jesus, my Savior, I pray the world wakes up to Your mission of love. Amen

God is Awesome, Say Amen

* After each "AMEN", if you agree with the prayer preceding it, say Amen out loud.

Glory Hallelujah!!! Jesus Christ is Risen from the dead. You are so awesome! AMEN

The melancholy of the Lenten season has lifted again this year to a renewed life of magnificent colors. A life forever not only for You, Lord, but also for me. Your pain has given way to the gift of eternal life for all humanity. A life filled with an amazing rainbow of colors; of harmony with all creatures; of expanding knowledge and of knowing we are loved. Wow! God, You did all this for us. Why then, is it too much for us to respect Your name, God, to keep it special?. AMEN

With the help of the Holy Spirit, I pray that I follow Your examples of kindness, acceptance and speaking harmonious thoughts instead of rumor, gossip and deceit. AMEN

With the help of the Holy Spirit, I pray that world leaders will work for peace; that children will be fed and healthy. I pray that no one will be oppressed by someone abusing whatever power they may have. Easter is a celebration of the absolute power of love to overcome any obstacle. I want to be part of the parade that is doing the will of God. I want to wave banners of peace and blanket those in need with caring. I want to sing *Beautiful Savior* and walk with determined faithfulness. AMEN

I confess that I am in need of forgiveness. I am sorry for my hang-ups and emotional dysfunctions. Thanks, God for Your forgiveness. I will also forgive those who have ticked me off- again and again. AMEN

As I gaze on the natural beauty of the Spring blossoms dressing the earth in celebration of Easter; I pray I will be committed to taking care of the earth and all living creatures. AMEN

Life is a journey of choices. Holy Spirit please guide me to make the right ones. AMEN

I pray for the blessings of hope and healing to_____.

Although I miss them, I am thankful for the loved ones in my life who are already spending eternity with You in Heaven. AMEN

In the name of my Risen Savior, Jesus Christ, the will of God be done in all things. AMEN

Jesus is Alive
Luke 24:1-9

Jesus Christ is Risen today. Jesus is alive!!! He lives for my family; He lives for soldiers; He lives for patients in nursing homes; He lives for kings, teachers, pastors and truck drivers. Christ is alive to be near me in this life and the next. Glory Hallelujah! What a positive power love is! Let my heart always be prepared to receive the gifts of bread and wine with a grateful heart and a sincere commitment of faith. I am sorry for my shortcomings- the sins of my actions and the sins of my silence. I pray that my church will be a beacon in the community and a place where people will feel welcome, safe and inspired to grow in their faith. I pray for the military- especially those who are away from their families in foreign lands where each day they face dangerous risks. Lord, I pray for their safe return. Thank You, Lord for Your saving grace. I accept Your love and the gift of eternal life. I pray for the youth living in my community. I pray churches find the energy and means to develop a youth ministry that is both fun and inspiring. Thank you Lord, for the beautiful music that stirs my soul to greater heights. Bless the musicians who give a good share of their time and their talent to worship You. I pray for Your children who must worship You in secret. Holy Spirit move among inmates in prisons and help those with addictions to have moments of clarity. I pray the lonely and isolated gain hope and find purpose for their lives. Lord, I pray for the ill and the grieving. I pray for those who are ready to begin their final journey. Let there be peace for them and their families. I pray especially for_____. Thank You again for Your sacrifice, grace and my redemption. In all things Your will be done. I pray all of these things in the name of Jesus AMEN.

The Boulder Moved and Jesus made His Exit from the Dead
Luke 23: 32-43

Glory Hallelujah! The boulder moved and Jesus made His exit from the dead. The tomb is empty! Jesus is risen- risen from the dead. Jesus, You are more alive than ever. Because of You, we are more alive with love, kindness and joy. Because You live- We will live- and not just in the present- We will share eternity with You in union with all the beautiful people who touch us in this world. Thank You for Your sacrifice to make it all possible. You have taken the sting out of death. Instead, we will be taking a journey without the baggage of pain, disappointment, guilt, loneliness and an array of unresolved issues. We will be free and unfettered to be the best we can be- a place to realize our goals without the hassle. Lord, help me to consider the beauty of Your creation each day and to contemplate how even more awesome it will be to spend an eternity with You in a place of even greater splendor. Will the butterflies and rainbows be enhanced with colors not visible on earth? Holy Spirit, guide Christians on this Easter day as we worship You in prayer, music and word. On this most Holy of days, I pray for peace. I pray for those, who like the thief on the cross, are remembered and are in the presence of our savior, Jesus Christ. In all things, I pray, in the name of Jesus, our Savior that Your purpose will be accomplished. Amen

GLORY HALLELUJIA JESUS, YOU ARE ALIVE.

Thank You Father. It was Your love for mankind that allowed the events of Holy Week to happen. It must have been horrible for You to see Your son experience his pain, humiliation and undeserved death. Because of You, death is an incredible new beginning. Help me to glance every day on the reality of eternity. Chatting with You now is a peek of my future with You. Holy Spirit, provide me with a life full of energy and purpose.

I pray for prodigal children who have drifted from their families and You. May they catch a glimpse of clarity to see what they are missing. May there always be hope for their families that they will return.

On this most holy of days, I pray for peace:

Peace in families
Peace in neighborhoods
Peace among nations
Peace within myself and Let the peace begin with me.

Lord, You showed mankind how to give of ourselves with the ultimate rewards that follow. As I give to others, I forget my own relatively insignificant problems. I pray for those who need to be close to You during difficult times in their lives- I pray for _____.
May they know they are loved by You and many others including me. Thank You, Jesus for becoming one of us! Amen

THE ASCENSION OF JESUS
Going Home
Luke 24:45-53

Greetings Father, Jesus and Holy Spirit. Today I celebrate and reflect about the time that Jesus was lifted up and went home. You went home after many major struggles on this earth. What a glorious day that must have been. Life has no meaning until death makes sense- Yours and mine. It is You, Lord, who makes sense out of death and You, Holy Spirit, who helps us to understand the meaning and purpose of life. Thank you. Amen

PENTECOST

Get the Kinks Out
Acts 2:4

Holy Spirit, You have been sent here to get the kinks out of our souls. I pray I listen to Your constructive advise and change some of my negative habits. People of all nations, languages and cultures understand the love You have for them and the joy of knowing Christ as their Savior. I pray that when You call me, Holy Spirit, I feel the warmth of Your flame encouraging me to be A disciple of Jesus and that I pay attention to Your guidance as I journey through life. Your will be done through me. Amen

REFORMATION DAY

God's Grace Saves and Changes Us
Romans 3: 19-28 John 8:31-36

God of all creation- No matter what the weather, today is a beautiful day to praise You. Fall is the season of rich oranges, browns, yellows and reds and the time for harvest. Thank You for the taste of pumpkin, apples, cider and the beer that the great reformer, Martin Luther, was so fond of.

Thinking of Martin Luther, I don't want to take Your grace for granted. Your grace saves us and then grace changes us. I pray that each day I am re-formed to know my true self. The self of having Jehovah dwelling within me. I am a diamond in the rough. Your grace brings out the luster and brilliance that I am capable of showing to the world by serving You and others. When I accept that God is dwelling in me, I will find my true self. Lord, I pray that there be renewal- a reformation of the church universal as we all seek the truth that will make us free. Free to search for truth without being bogged down by strict traditions and limiting exclusive theologies. You include sinners into your circle of love. I pray that I will also be accepting. After all, Heaven is not a "gated community" reserved for any specific denomination. Thank You, Lord, for the abundance in my life as I enjoy the colors, tastes and smells of the earth shedding summer and churning once again to a season known for harvesting the fruit of the earth and our labor. Lord, I pray for those who are lonely, grieving, abused, alienated, unemployed or ill. Please heal and comfort_____. Your unconquerable heart of love will always be stronger than death. Holy Spirit, please guide my journey of being a role model of Your love and grace to those who seek Your truth. In the name of Jesus, I pray Your will be done in churches, temples and mosques and wherever people of faith gather. Amen

MOTHER'S DAY

God's Wings .....

In honor of Mother's day, I would like to share a story called, *God's Wings*. You may also have seen this email.

After a forest fire in Yellowstone National Park, forest rangers began their trek up a mountain to assess the inferno's damage. One ranger found a bird literally petrified in ashes, perched statuesquely on the ground at the base of a tree. When he gently struck it, three tiny chicks scurried from under their dead mother's wings.

The loving mother, keenly aware of impending disaster, had carried her offspring to the base of the tree and had gathered them under her wings, instinctively knowing that the toxic smoke would rise. She could have flown to safety but had refused to abandon her babies. When the blaze had arrived and the heat had scorched her small body, the mother had remained steadfast....because she had been willing to die, so those under the cover of her wings would live. 'He will cover you with His feathers, And under His wings you will find refuge.' ~ Psalm 91:4

Lord, this is a day we honor mothers. Help me to be a blessing to my mom and not to take her for granted. I can show her I care and appreciate her with a hug or a phone call. Lord, also bless the mothers who have transitioned to being grandmothers. May their joy increase as they pass their life lessons on to precious grandchildren. Thank You, Lord for being a foundational part of their life and of mine. Thank You for my mother. I pray Your will be done within families of all types including single parent, stepparent, adoptive and foster families. Amen

Jesus Loved His Mother

Lord, today is Mother's Day. It is a day to celebrate mothers. Jesus, You loved Your mother very much. She was a blessed woman and became a blessing to You. Jesus, I am thankful for Your mother, Mary, who nurtured You as a child, who supported You in Your destiny, who grieved Your death and rejoiced when You resurrected to a higher realm of existence. Mary remains a blessing to Christians worldwide.

Bless mothers as they nurture their children with loving hearts. My heart goes out to mothers who helplessly hold seriously ill children in their laps or grieve the loss of a child. Be with the many mothers who have a child or a husband in the military. Peace, let there be peace to bring loved ones home to their waiting mothers.. Bless the mothers who cast their smiles from above as they are embraced in Your presence. Help me to be a blessing to my Mom and to not take her for granted. I can show her I care and appreciate her with a hug or a phone call. Thank You, God, for my mother. May Your will be done within families of all nations, cultures and religions. Amen

Grandparents Day–National Grandparents Day is the first Sunday of September after Labor Day

Young at Heart

Today is Grandparent's Day. I pray for grandparents as they share their time, values and faith with their grandchildren. Grandchildren bless and enrich the lives of grandparents in very special ways which encourage a young at heart attitude. Grandparents are also a blessing by confirming how valued and special their grandchildren are to them. I pray especially for the over 2 million courageous grandparents in this country who are raising their grandchildren as custodial parents. I am thankful for my Grandmas and Grandpas. Lord, I pray that I am or will be a playful grandparent and that I am a grateful grandchild. In the name of Jesus, Your will be done in the lives of grandparents. Amen

Lord, Bless Grandmothers
Contributed by Chantal Woods

Dear Lord I ask that you bless all grandmother's, and let them be in great health and happiness. I ask that you let them forever be our sunshine.

LABOR DAY

Labor Day–Your Truth Is Marching On
(Inspired by the Battle Hymn of the Republic)

Glory, Glory Hallelujah, Your truth is marching on. This is a difficult time for many people in the USA. In the midst of finger pointing, blaming and excuses, I pray prosperity and leadership with integrity marches forward with a plan of renewal for people challenged by unemployment, rising prices and a roller coaster stock market. I pray for families to have faith in You and each other. With faith, there is hope for the future. I pray my family is inspired by the flame of Your truth. Lord, I pray that Your truth will march on in schools so that Your values will be learned alongside of history, math and social studies so that students learn to be a success as a person as well as with a career. May Your truth march on with me as I meditate in prayer and when I share my faith with others. Glory glory hallelujah. Your truth is marching on in the workplaces of America. In the name of Jesus, I pray for prosperity. Amen

Labor Less Day

This is a Selah prayer. After each Selah, pause a moment to think about what you just prayed or continue on in prayer to God.

Lord, where has the summer gone? School has started and our Fall activities and schedules are beginning to fill up our calendars and time. In preparation, we celebrate Labor Day. Maybe it should be called Labor Less Day. So this weekend I will labor less and take time to relax. I will take time to breath slowly and deeply while breathing in the presence of the Holy Spirit and then breathing out positive thoughts for self and others. *Selah*

Lord, I am thankful for all the successes in my life. Success, however, without a sense of wonder does not embrace the "Big Picture". Holy Spirit, please help me to see the big picture. *Selah*

As students return to school, I pray that parents are involved in their children's education. I pray that positive values are taught along with math English and science. I pray that students are encouraged to become curious, creative and confident. *Selah*

God, You are magnificent! You are here and now- in all places- at all times- with all people. I don't have to die to get a glimpse of heaven. S*elah*

There are friends and family who are facing challenges in their life. I lift up in prayer_____

Oh Lord, the world news is violently scary. I pray for peace. Peace in homes, Peace in America and Peace worldwide. *Selah*

Lord, I won't forget to take time for You this weekend. I will begin with Psalm 46:10

Be still and know that I am God
Be still and know that I am
Be still and know
Be still
Be

PATRIOTIC PRAYERS

Memorial Day–God of Our Fathers
Isaiah 12:2-6

Dear God of our Fathers and of all those who played their part in shaping America. Our forefathers founded this land of the free in Your name. I pray that the United States of America stand true to the values of those who gave their limbs and lives for freedom. I also pray for all the veterans who have served in wars and conflicts...especially the vets whose bodies and minds are permanently damaged and residing in veteran hospitals. I pray for the safety of all military personnel. I pray for those in power, who in the safety of their homes and offices, make decisions about war and send young parents or loved children to do the dirty work of war. Holy Spirit, please enlighten world leaders to promote and choose peaceful methods of solving global problems- at least to strive with all their might to explore other alternatives besides military action. I pray for the men and women who are serving today in war torn countries plagued with irrational dictators, extremists and terrorists. I pray for their safety as our military personnel defend helpless citizens while also promoting good will. Be with them as they go about their daily duties in foreign lands. I pray they return safely to their families. In the name of Jesus, I pray for world peace. Amen

Memorial Day–I Pledge Allegiance

I pledge allegiance to my God who is all powerful- who believes in peace.

I pledge allegiance to my God who mourns death and destruction resulting from war.

I pledge allegiance to my God who is with the men and women who are serving our country. I pray they will soon return home to their families. I remember the veterans who have given their lives, limbs and mental health in the name of war. It is good to know that lives lost can be found in Your presence. Holy Spirit, please enlighten world leaders to promote and choose peaceful methods of solving global problems. Your will be done in all nations.

I pledge allegiance to my country as I take advantage of the free-doms allowed in a democracy. Freedom that I can't take for granted because it came at a very high price. I need to reflect on the respon-sibilities that freedoms are dependent on. I pray the polluted waters flooding the values of people and nations recede. The power of prayer can change each of us to see Your truth as clearly as I can see the beauty of Your creation on a sunny day. When I gaze out at Lake Erie, *(or other large body of water)* it also reminds me of Your love. I can see the beginning but not the end. Let peace begin with me. Amen

Memorial Day Tribute
II Corinthians 2: 14-15

The tribute below is a reflection of Randy Nickel, Young Life International Outreach Director

In the US the last Monday of the month of May is a national hol-iday called Memorial Day. It is a day that is set aside to remember those men and women in the armed services that have given their life in service to their country. Each town typically has a parade or a memorial service to honor those that have fallen protecting our country.

Yesterday, I took Joy, a friend of hers and my dog Sammy up town so we could see the parade. The parade has the high school marching band, police, firefighters, fire trucks, city council, the mayor, boy scout troops, and veterans from various wars. It was a beautiful morning and the crowds were out. As I stood by the street a man was walking down the street. He was about 60 or 65 years old. He was wearing his old uniform. I could tell by what he wore that he fought in Vietnam. He was carrying a stack of photocopies a few hundred thick. He walked up to me and introduced himself. I thanked him for his service to our county. He thanked me and then said that the reason he was here though was to give people a sheet of paper. He said it highlighted his best friend who was a true hero. He told me that his friend never made it home from the war and he did not want his friend to be forgotten. I was instantly choked up. I thought of many of my closest friends and wondered would I do the same for them 45 years later. I took the paper and thanked him.

The story was amazing. His friend died in 1969. His unit walked into an ambush and a fire fight ensued. He was shot in the arm. He continued to shoot with his opposite arm until he was shot in that arm as well. He then ran to draw fire away from his buddies so they could escape. He ran with no ability to shoot back knowing that he would probably die. As you can tell I was very moved. As I thought about doing that for my friends another thought hit me. Jesus did the exact same thing for us. He was willing to die in our place. He is a hero for people all over the world. Do I have the same intensity and passion to share this with others so they do not forget that loving sacrifice? This man did not care what others thought he just wanted to make sure his friend was not forgotten. May we have the same passion. The thought of losing one of my sons is overwhelming. What would it mean to me if years later his friends were making sure his memory was not forgotten? I would be so grateful. I believe God the Father feels the same when we tell others about his son. He is pleased that we remember His Son and what He did for us. I think it brings a smile to God's face and a tear to His eye.

May we never forget to appreciate the ultimate sacrifice men and women have given in war torn countries. Thank you wherever you are.

Unknown Soldiers Prayer
Galatians 5: 12-15

The poem below was in a newspaper clipping saved in my aunt's Bible in the 1940's. It was originally found on the body of an unknown soldier during WWII. Since the Revolutionary War that forged our freedom, there have been many more battles resulting in the sacrifice of known and unknown soldiers. I have since seen versions of this in email format, however I never forgot when my aunt shared this poem with me.

I asked God for strength that I might achieve-
I was made weak, that I might learn humbly to obey.
I asked for health that I might do greater things-
I was given infirmity that I might do better things
I asked for riches that I might be happy-
I was given poverty that I might be wise.
I asked for power that I might have the praise of men-
I was given weakness that I might feel the need of God.
I asked for all things that I might enjoy life
I was given life that I might enjoy all things.
I got nothing that I asked for
But everything I had hoped for.

"Let Freedom Ring" is still burning in the hearts of people today. I pray that freedom becomes a reality for them. Till then...I also pray for the inward freedom of their minds and souls. Thank You God that I live in a free country where I can speak my mind and share my faith in You without fear. With all its imperfections, America is still a great nation. Lord, I pray for the safe return of our military to their families. I pray they leave behind positive footprints and memories. Lord, comfort those who are weary with stress, grief and illness- especially_____ Glory hallelujah!! God bless America! In the name of Jesus, let there be peace! AMEN.

My Country tis of You, Lord

This prayer is inspired by the hymn, My Country tis of Thee
VERSE 1: FREEDOM

God of all nations and all people- I thank You that I live in a free nation- free to worship and sing Your praises whenever and wherever I want to. Lord, never let me take this freedom for granted. I remember on this day that my freedom came with a cost. The cost of lives and disabled minds and bodies. Although America has important issues to deal with I am fortunate and blessed the be a citizen of the USA. Lord I would rather be a problem solver than part of the problem.

Lord, let freedom ring throughout the world. Holy Spirit, move world leaders to accept peace, allow freedom of faith and promote dignity to all individuals. Until then, I pray for Your followers and disciples who worship You in secret, in prison or are persecuted for loving You. Yes, this is still happening today. From every mountainside and every shore let freedom ring. God bless America

Verse 2: FOOD, LAND and ENVIRONMENT

Lord, when You created this world, You did it right! The earth has an abundance- an over abundance of resources to feed, clothe and shelter every family. Lord, motivate individuals and nations to share their knowledge and resources. By world standards, I am rich. Lord, inspire me to share my wealth and to become involved with a cause that alleviates suffering. The trees of our land whisper sweet music in the breeze. The music of the leaves is one of Your soothing creations that I appreciate.

I am sorry that in so many ways we deface the earth You created by littering the land as well as spilling sewage and toxic chemicals into rivers, lakes and oceans. I wonder. Is defacing Your art work less important than defacing treasured paintings of Da Vinci or Monet with magic marker graffiti? I will recycle more and litter less. God bless America

Verse 3: WORK and MINISTRY of the CHURCH

Lord, protect and expand the ministry of _____, and the service projects of _____. Bless Mission Teams with the help of the Holy Spirit as they prepare for their journeys to share their faith to people who need to know and love You, Lord. I pray for Teen Shelters, Habitat for Humanity, Food Pantry's, Domestic Violence Shelters and Homeless Programs that my faith community supports. I pray for those who visit congregational members in need. I pray for Pastors, support staff and volunteers who make congregations vital and caring. God bless America and _____ (My local community)

Verse 4: PRAYER for NEEDS

I pray for Your children for whom the night is lonely and tempests rage. I pray for healing of body, mind and soul- I lift up____*names*_____ for Your healing touch. With Your great might, God bless America Amen

If this prayer is used in a church setting,- a soloist or the congregation can sing the verses of 'My Country Tis of Thee' when noted in the prayer.

Independence Day–God of our Ancestors

God, You are Creator–Shepherd -Savior–Lover of all humanity–Dad–Holy–Almighty–God of my ancestors and all who have followed. From the first Adams and Eves You created them free. Free the way You meant them to be. I wonder, Lord, are Christians the only ones who disrespect the name of their god? If we think You are so awesome, if we believe in You; if we think You are worthy of our worship; if we know Jesus Christ is our savior and we will live forever in Your presence...then why oh why do Christians use Your name in such disrespectful ways? Do You wince every time someone says or emails OMG or cuss in Your name? I need to remember that with freedom comes responsibility for what I speak and for my actions. Thank You, my God, that I live in a free country where I can speak my mind and share my faith in You without fear. I pray for those who are less fortunate. "Let Freedom Ring" is still burning in the hearts of people today. Until freedom becomes a reality for them, I pray for inward freedom of their minds and souls. I pray for missionaries worldwide who are serving You. Holy Spirit move like the wind to inspire, encourage and clarify Your truth in all languages. Empower the souls of Your faithful who speak of Your love to teens, to the grieving and dying, to the addicted, to the isolated, to those with mental illness and to criminals. May the positive footprints and accepting smiles of missionaries be a lasting memory in the lives of needful people. I pray for the safe return of our military who continue to serve as well as the safety of our police and firefighters. May they all promote peace abroad and at home in the USA. An angel thank you to those who served in a freedom revolution. 1776 was a very good year for America. God bless America. In the name of Jesus, Your will be done in all things and with me. Amen

God Bless America

My county tis of You, Lord- a sweet land of liberty. I am so thankful that this land of freedom was founded in Your name and that our fore-fathers were not ashamed to declare their allegiance to You, God. I pray that I follow in their footsteps. I can respectfully acknowledge the faith of others. I can also stand up for You as the cornerstone of both my life and the United States. God bless America. With all of its imperfections it is still the best place for me to live and worship You. Let freedom always ring true in this beautiful land of lakes and trees and children playing on swings. I pray for our economy. Please help America be a country where people can earn an honest living and live on what they earn. As individuals and as a country may we learn from our mistakes and united grow stronger after adversity. I pray that local and federal political leaders make common sense decisions and laws with fairness for all. Thank You, God, for the abundance of natural resources and diverse beauty of this land Americans call home. God bless America. Your will be done in this land.

In Memory of 9/11 Twin Tower Tragedy
John 6:33

Lord, You are awesome! Thank You for directing my life in so many ways- ways that I am often not aware of. I pray that my soul is lifted toward You during my prayer and that I will listen to the whispers of inspiration from the Holy Spirit. In memory of the 9/11 tragedy, I pray for the survivors and for the families and loved ones of those who did not survive. Was it fate or Your intervention that saved some of the survivors? People are alive today because of life's little annoy-ances. Some of the little things in life made a huge difference on that fatal day.

Some reasons people survived 9/11 are:

The head of a company survived 9/11 because his son started kindergarten.

Another man is alive because it was his turn to bring donuts.
A woman was late because her alarm did not go off in time.
One or more were late because of being stuck on the NJ Turnpike
because of an accident.
One missed the bus
One had to change clothes because of spilling food.
A car would not start
Someone went back to answer the phone
A mom's child dawdled

And there was the man who put on a new pair of shoes. Before
getting to work, he got a blister so stopped at the drugstore to buy a
Band-Aid. Because of a Band-Aid, he survived 9/11. Those who did
not survive are still missed. Holy Spirit, please comfort their families and help them to see the big picture of everlasting life and that
someday they will be reunited. Lord, help me to remember that when
I can't find my car keys or I'm stuck in traffic or when any number of
annoying things happen, You, my dear God, are watching over me.
I pray for peace. Let peace begin with me. Amen

Veteran's Day–With Freedom Comes Responsibility
Galatians 5:1

Dear God of our fathers and forefathers, thank You for our Freedoms.
I need to remember that with freedom comes responsibility. By Your
grace, Christ has set us free. We are free to worship You, however,
we need to stand firm in our right to express our faith in You. Mary
lost her son to the cause of spiritual freedom. Uncountable American
mothers in generations of wars have lost their sons for people of all
faiths and denominations to celebrate, Christmas, Hanukah, Kwanza,
Ramadan and other religious anniversaries. Lord, I will not take for
granted Your sacrifice and the sacrifices of Your children. Lord, I
pray for sons and daughters now in the military who continue the
fight of our forefathers for freedom. Continue to bless them, Lord,

when they return home. Lord, I pray 'The Church' will be a beacon of hope in our communities that also stretches beyond our borders as we give of ourselves in service to others and as we share our faith in You Lord. Lord, I pray comfort of body, mind and spirit be felt to those in need. I pray especially for....................

Lord, I need Your help with.................. It took God a week to make the earth and stars; the moon, Jupiter and Mars. How special I must be because, God, You are still working on me. God, bless the Vets! In all things, Your will be done Amen.

Let Freedom Ring

God of all nations and all people- I thank You that I live in a free nation- free to worship and sing Your praises whenever and wherever I want to. Lord, never let me take this freedom for granted and to always remember, that my freedom comes with a cost. The cost of lives as well as disabled minds and bodies. Lord, let freedom ring throughout the world. Holy Spirit, move world leaders to promote peace. Until then, I pray for Your followers and disciples, who worship You in secret because they are persecuted for loving You. From every mountainside and every shore let freedom ring. The earth has an abundance- an over abundance of resources to feed, clothe and shelter every family. Lord, motivate individuals and nations to share their knowledge and resources. By world standards, I am rich so Lord, inspire me to share my wealth and to become involved with a cause that alleviates suffering. I pray for Your children for whom the night is lonely and tempests rage. I pray they find comfort, acceptance and purpose as veterans and their families struggle when they return home after their traumatic experiences abroad. In all things, Your will be done in the name of Jesus. Amen

CHILDREN

Prayer on the Birth of a Child
Matthew 19:13-15

Glory Hallelujah! Lord, I am filled with pure joy on the birth of__ *baby's name*____. I am so thankful this beautiful child has arrived to share his/her life with God and family. The birth of a child is one of life's greatest miracles. ____mom's name____, _dad's name_____ and You sure did good. Lord, I know You are sharing in my smiles as I hold and gaze on _baby's name_____. Loving a child together, helps me to understand You more and deepens our relationship. I feel closer to You as I share the love in my heart for this precious child who is also a child of Yours.. Lord, keep __baby's name_____ in Your lap so that she/he will learn about Your love. Holy Spirit, inspire ___baby's name___ soul throughout his/her life to know the truth of Your essence and her/his purpose in this life. Jesus, I know that children are special to you. You gathered them in Your arms and blessed them. I pray that this child will always know how much You love him/her. Throughout his/her life, please keep __baby's name_____ safe from those who would do harm or try to lure her/him from a relationship with You. Thank You ever so much for the adorable addition to my family. Guide me to be a positive role model _baby's name___will look up to and respect. I love You and want to share that love with my family. In the name of Jesus, I pray that _baby's name____be blessed and be a blessing. Amen

Is Abba "Dad" in Hebrew?

Greetings Father God- One name You were called by Jesus, was Abba.. Some theological scholars think the Hebrew translation for Abba is "Dad". I like that translation. Children will especially feel You are more approachable. What a joy children are. I know You love them with gusto.

I pray for children- especially those in distress because of illness, family circumstances or poverty. There are many hungry children in this world. I also pray with joy for the children who are baptized with water and the word. I pray parents keep their baptismal promise to teach their children to know You, Father. I pray for a gazillion bless-ings on *name of child/children* as *name/names* grows in stature and faith. We can see the children as they are now in the beginning of their life but we have yet to see the end as they mature into an adult child of God.

. Thinking of You in the more casual term of Dad rather than Father also helps me to feel more comfortable talking with You. Dads are playful so we can share fun times and silly thoughts together. May Your will be done in the lives of children worldwide. Amen

God Loves Children John 3:16

This prayer is mostly for children, however, parents can pray along with their child/children. You know, you don't have to pray all the time with your eyes closed. Sometimes having our eyes closed helps us so we don't get distracted by stuff. Another choice is to look at a cross as you pray. Today we are just going to talk to God.

Thank You God for loving me so much. I love You too. Thank You for loving me and caring about me even when I get in trouble. Thank You for my family.

God bless children who don't have enough to eat or are sick. I will try to help other children if they are sad and need a friend. I will share some of my toys and games when I play with other kids. I don't want to be a bully. Instead, I will be a friend to someone who is being bullied. God bless all the lonely children because they don't have friends or they miss a family member who is not around any-more. God bless my teachers in school and Sunday School because they help me to learn important information and how to be a better person. God bless my family, my friends and all the people who make me happy and keep me safe. God bless the people that need You to comfort them.

Help me to know You better and to keep learning about You as I grow up. You are my friend, I'm Your friend. Amen

Back to School

Lord, I pray for students and teachers returning for another school year. I pray that this be a positive year of learning and expanding horizons. There are so many opportunities for teachers to inspire and encourage students from all walks of life. I pray for students- especially those away at college. Lord keep them safe physically and spiritually. There are so many ways the vulnerable can be tempted. As our college students return to school, I pray they won't party too hardy. As they are exposed to new philosophies, ideologies and theologies I pray the search for truth leads students to an even stronger conviction of God's presence in their lives. I pray they will be curious to learn and that they find a goal worth pursuing that will maintain their interest for years to come in their future vocations. Holy Spirit be with the leaders of campus ministry to inspire and encourage students of faith and as they introduce Jesus to other students knocking on the door to God's presence in their lives. Your will be done in classrooms, locker rooms and dormitories. Amen

Children's Prayer–So Long School and Hello Summer

*Kids, this prayer is for you....*Open hands, palms up- invite God into your spiritual heart.

Thank You, God that I made it through another year at school and that I live in a place where I can go to school. I feel sorry for the children who can't go to school because they are too sick or live in a country where lots of children don't go to school. Dear God, help them in any way that You can. God, I will miss seeing some of my friends over the summer. I hope they will by OK and have a nice summer. I hope I will have a nice summer with my family too. God, sometimes I don't understand why bad things happen to good people who don't deserve it. Like, bad things happened to Jesus too. I'm glad Jesus is OK now. God bless and please help children and their families who have bad things happen to them. God, be with all our police officers and firefighters. God, I want to keep learning more about You and get to know You better. God, help me to be a good person. I want to tell the truth, to be kind, to be helpful and to care about other people's feelings. God please bless my family, my friends and bless my pet. God, You are my friend. God bless Yourself and me. Amen

Villages Raise Children
Deuteronomy 6:4-7

Dear Father You love us all so deeply. I am blessed to be Your child. Every child on earth is in Your loving care as You shed tears of joy and pain for them. Since I don't see the whole picture, sometimes it is hard for me to understand the suffering some children experience. Holy Spirit, help me to understand. Guide me to help make a difference in their lives. I pray that the Holy Spirit move, as only the Holy Spirit can, to enlighten students who are seeking a relationship with You. Lord, they need Your truth as our world seems to be infested with weeds of self destructive values expanding more out of control each year as those weeds are fertilized by the media to normalize and glorify reckless behavior. Lord, I pray for children who have turned their hurt into anger. I pray for children who are hungry, in pain and who suffer from neglect and abuse. I pray for children who are ill- especially in places where medical care is not available. God, bless and give help to social workers, medical staff and volunteers responding with love to the needs of Your children. Let there be hope for a better life. I pray for students in Universities being exposed to new (for them) philosophies, theologies and values which can ignite seeds of doubt. Holy Spirit, please guide their search for truth to lead them to a closer relationship with You and a faith with more conviction. I also pray that they don't lose sight of their goals. In the name of Jesus, I pray for all children to have seeds of faith in You that will grow and blossom . Amen

Prayer for Christian Educators and Students.
John 14: 25-26

I am thankful for the inspiration and guidance of the Holy Spirit. Holy Spirit, work Your wonders so that we all are under God's spell stirring our spiritual nature to see God more clearly. I pray for Sunday School teachers. Holy Spirit, guide them and inspire them to teach about Your love and forgiveness with truth and joy. May they have fun as teachers of Your Word. As they teach, may they also learn. If I fit into this picture by helping in any way, guide me to do so. I pray for the children of the world who are young in their faith. May their faith grow, blossom and become strong enough to weather the storms that will come their way and the temptations they will be confronted with. I pray for students who need You close to them for physical, mental and spiritual healing. I pray for..................... I pray in the name of Jesus that every day, we all be under God's spell of a faith that never stops maturing, learning and loving. Amen

Healthy, Happy and Full of Love– A Bedtime Prayer for Children

This is a different take on the traditional prayer I learned as a child which I changed when I became a parent. I wanted a more positive prayer for my children to pray before going to sleep.

The last line can be increased in volume with each word.

This prayer should be said with a smile. After being said, the child can say God bless to whomever they want.

Now I lay you down to sleep
I pray O Lord our* child to keep.
Your love guard _child's name_ through the night.
And wake her/him with the morning light. Healthy, Happy and Full of Love!

* *'our' refers to the child being both God's and your child*

God's Son Visits Earth–Prayer for A Children's Christmas Program

Since this is a children's service, I will be leading the children in prayer. Adults can listen in–OK kids, let's talk with God.

Thank You, God, for allowing Your son to visit people on earth. It is amazing, Jesus, that You choose to enter the world NOT as a soldier, a king or a superhero. You chose to arrive as a baby in a barn. Thank You, Jesus for choosing to become a child so You could totally understand what it is like for me growing up. I think You must love animals because animals were among the first to welcome Your birth. I like animals too. Well, most of them. Some should stay outside in nature where they like it best. People need to protect the endangered animals because all animals have a purpose. I am waiting to celebrate Your Birthday on Christmas Day. As my parents, grandmas and grandpas get ready for Your Birthday, I need to remember that although presents are great, I need to also think about gifts I can give. (Like helping pick up, saying, "thank you", sharing a toy, coloring a picture for someone) Whenever I make someone feel good, that is a gift to them. King Herod only wanted control and things. The angels gave Jesus beautiful music. The Shepherds gave Jesus their hearts full of love. The Wise men gave Jesus some things He would need in the future when Jesus became an adult. The Wise men also gave Jesus their Faith—faith that Jesus would someday become their teacher and savior. Whenever I talk to God, I am giving God a gift. God, You love me when I am naughty and You love me when I an nice. Thank You God, for loving me all the time. God bless all the people who are sick or hurting in any way. God bless my family and friends. God bless my teachers. God bless the soldiers who wish they could be home for Christmas. Merry Christmas Jesus! I'll talk to You again soon. Amen

CHILDREN'S LESSONS

Lessons for children when combined with a visual aid are more relevant for young minds and will be more memorable. With a little imagination, everyday objects can be used to explain some pretty deep ideas, values and their relationship with God. I could do a book just of Children's lessons or sermons. For now, I have included a few outlines of Children's lessons that can be expanded on; the more spontaneous the presentation the better. If you teach Sunday School or give children's sermons I hope you will be inspired to go crazy fun teaching kids about God's love.

Children's Lesson–I've got the Power

"HeMan: Masters of the Universe" was a TV Super Hero in the 1980s—before you were born. Like many superheroes, HeMan was a shy normal person until someone was in serious trouble. He had a special sword that he would lift to the sky and then say, "By the power of Gray Skull, I've got the power." Then magically, shy prince Adam would become a bold super hero to save his kingdom from evil Skeletor and other bad guys. They can be related to bullies, drug dealers, sickness, hunger, etc. It was a cool TV series that had a moral to each story. A moral is a way to be a better person. HeMan had helpers like Cringer/Battle Cat and Orko.

Jesus was also a super hero before you were born. He was born as a normal baby and grew up just like you are growing up in a nice family. Jesus also has a special power; the power of His father, God. With the power of God's love, Jesus could do love miracles like healing people of illness, sadnness and lonliness.. Jesus has the power to help people deal with the bad things that happen to them. Yep, even the baddest of the bad. Because of Jesus, we will never die. Instead, we will be transformed—wonderfully changed—to live forever. Jesus also had helpers called disciples who learned the truth of God's love and shared that truth with thousands of people. We are still being called by God to be kind, to be honest and to help people in need. The story of Jesus still needs to be told.

There are lots of pretend super heroes like Superman, Spiderman and He Man but the real super hero is Jesus.

Dirty Bowl
Matthew 6:1-6, 16-18

Props: A dirty bowl on both the inside and outside: with food, mud or whatever. Optional: wash cloth or paper towels two bowls-one dirty and one clean

This can be a talk on priorities and the really important values in life.

We are the dish. Is it more important for the outside of the bowl to be clean and pretty with a fancy design on it or is more important for the inside of the bowl to be clean?

- *As you wipe the dirt off the outside:* It is not wrong to have the outside of the bowl to be clean or to have a design, however, there is so much more to our being than the clothes we wear, how smart we are or how many toys we have. Our faith in God is so much more than just going to Sunday School and church.
- *As you wipe the dirt off the inside:* The inside of the bowl is about our faith in God and how we treat others. It is more important to share than to have scads of toys or expensive clothes. It is just as or more important to learn about God as it is to learn about math and science.
- Think about whether you want to be clean on the inside by being kind, generous etc. or being pretty on the outside with fancy clothes you will outgrow or wear out.

Solid Wood

Prop: A log like one used in a fireplace and some smaller branches and twigs
Theme: The log is a symbol of being a faith filled person.

Norway is a very cold country. For hundreds of years, people depended on wood for their very survival. Wood was used to keep warm, build shelter, cook their meals and catch food with. Norwegians are well known as fisherman so they used wood to build their fishing boats. Even today it is hard to imagine living without good strong wood.

A man from Norway is called, 'Solid Wood', if he has good qualities. He practices his faith in God, is dependable, takes care of his family, is a loyal friend, and helps people in need. To call a Norwegian man, "Solid Wood" is a very high compliment. The log used to be a branch or twig. The branch grew to be a log. You are like the small branches growing into a log. As you make good choices and serve others in kindness, your log will grow in strength and stability.

A log strong enough for others to lean on and learn from.

Jesus, is our "Solid Wood". Jesus is dependable because He is the way to eternal life with God. He is a loyal friend that we can talk to in prayer. Jesus is not only our Savior, He helps and comforts us when we feel alone or fearful.

So by following Jesus we can grow to be "Solid Wood" as we serve others. Being "Solid Wood" is a good thing to be and for all of us to strive for. God helps us to be that kind of person.

Wash the Sin Away
John 13:1-17

Prop: Wash cloth and or towel

OUTLINE

How we use a wash cloth Explanation
- To soak up a spill -The spill is sin. Jesus wipes sin away.
- To apply polish-The Holy Spirit helps us to shine more brightly
- To pick up something hot/cold- God serves and speaks to people whose faith is hot and also to those whose faith is cold.
- To wrap something fragile-During difficult and challenging times when we are vulnerable God comforts us and helps us.
- To keep something warm-We all have times when we doubt/have questions about God. If we ask God for guidance and ask for help, we will be comforted and feel God's warm love. Your faith may then actually become stronger.
- As a tourniquet-Jesus is a life saver and He can stop the sin from spreading. When He died on the cross, we are saved.
- To clean-Jesus used the towel to serve by cleaning his disciples feet of dust and dirt because of wearing sandals in the streets. We are also called to serve by helping people.
- We can also be a washcloth to help others.

Dog Tag/Name Label

The inspiration for this lesson was formed when I came across my own dog tag. During WWII students were given dog tags which we wore to school. It was a time when schools not only had fire drills, we also had bomb drills.

Props: Dog tag and or a name label–Optional–Oriental Express has inexpensive dog tag style necklaces with a smiley face to give as an optional handout or each child could be given a name tag.

Theme: God does not need labels to know who we are.

• Dog tags are worn by the military in case they get lost or injured so the people who rescue them know who they are and who they need to contact.
• Some people wear medical alert tags that inform Doctors and emergency workers of a special need they have. Diabetic, heart condition, severe allergies etc.
• Name labels are used at meetings and parties to help people greet and meet each other.

God does not need any tags or labels to find us or to know who we are. If our dog tags are dirty or bent, God loves us just as we are and knows what we need. We are all God's children and he loves each of us. God knows what we need. God not only knows you from the outside, God knows who you are on the inside. He shares your fun times and your sad times. God enjoys knowing when you are kind, generous and gentle to people and also to animals.

GOD IS LIKE...

Props: A few items below or of your own choosing. There are other commercials that can also be used. You could also just pick one for a very brief lesson or as an add on to another lesson you are teaching. A few are for adults.

Bayer Aspirin: He works miracles
Ford: He's got a better idea
Coke: He's the real thing thing
Hallmark cards: He cares enough to send His very best
Tide: He gets the stains out that others leave behind
General Electric: He brings good things to life
Sears: He has everything
Alka Seltzer: Try Him, you'll like Him
Scotch Tape: You can't see Him, but you know He's there.
Delta: He's ready when you are.
Allstate: You're in good hands with Him
VO5 hair spray: He holds through all kinds of weather
Dial soap: Aren't you glad you have Him? Don't you wish everybody did?
Wheaties: God is the nourishment of champions
US Post Office: Neither rain nor snow nor sleet nor ice will keep Him from His appointed destination.
USA TV Channel: Characters welcome
Toshiba: He thought of everything
Ohio Wesleyan: Change your life, change the world.
Progressive Insurance: Sometimes it pays to switch things up.
Travelocity: You never roam alone
State Farm: Get to a better state
Assurance Wireless: A worry free way to stay connected
Febreze: Breath happy
SyFy TV channel: Imagine greater
Lowes: Build something better

Wire Walker

This lesson was inspired by watching Nik Wallenda cross the Grand Canyon on a tight rope.

Prop: A rope or cable 6 feet or longer–Have 2 children hold the rope; one at each end. You can ask them if they think you could walk the rope and then if any of them could walk on the rope. Hopefully you will get a few laughs or giggles.

Theme: God helps those who do their homework, practices the piano, and who practice and then play hard at their sport. If we want to excel at something or do something risky, we can't expect God to get us through without hard work on our part. God will, however, help us to do the seemingly impossible. Before Nik Wallenda does his incredible feats of wire walking, he does months of research and practices rigorously until he is confident that he can accomplish his goal. With all the practice and hard work, Nik knew he needed God at his side and had a running conversation thanking Jesus as he walked across the Grand Canyon.

LOLLYPOP

Props: bunch of lollypops to hand out. You can give each child 2 and ask them to share one.

Optional: cards or posters with a letter/word on each to spell lollypop (or lollipop as both are correct) You can draw just the letters on one side and the word on the back. That is especially helpful for the memory challenged to remember the words that go with each letter.

What makes a lollypop a lollypop?
Sugar candy = Jesus
Handle = Faith

Different Flavors and shapes of Lollypops Symbolize: Diversity and different shapes and shades of people and Christians of various Denominations/theology- All believe in Jesus

Take off the wrapper; Get to know Jesus -How sweet it is to know Jesus. Don't hide that you love Jesus "Hide it under a bushel? No"

Special Lollypops:
Each lollypop is special with unique gifts/talents. Jesus calls us to use them to serve others- sharing, music, being kind, helping family

and friends etc. If there are enough children have them line up to spell Lollypop . The first letter of each word spells LOLLYPOP. LOVE OFFER LEARN LIVE YES PRAY OPEN PARTY As each word is presented by the child, you can explain in one or two sentences what they mean as a Christian. Jesus loves us. Jesus offers us His friendship and eternal life. We want to learn more about Jesus and we can learn from Him on how to have a good life. Say YES to Jesus. Pray to Jesus. Open your heart to Jesus. Have a party because being a Christian is fun.

SHARING PRAYERS

Making Prayer Personal
When Praying With Someone

- Pray a silent prayer to the Holy Spirit to guide you in prayer.

- Make the prayer personal to God, to those you are praying for and to yourself.

- **To God:** Praise, Thanksgiving and Petition
- **To those you are praying for**. Use their names in the prayer. Be specific to their concerns and situation. Be positive with God's love, grace and understanding. Pray for not only physical healing, but also for emotional strength and spiritual growth. The more you know the person/persons you are praying with, the more personal the prayers can become. If appropriate, suggest you hold hands during the prayer. If you are using a Bible verse, you may want to incorporate the message into the prayer. Especially if there is some dementia- keep it simple. Pray with love in your heart and encouragement on your lips.

Regardless of the situation- including near death, there is hope because of God's saving grace. Even if not spoken, embrace the journey of everlasting life in God's presence. Death is not an ending- it is a transformation

3. **To yourself:** Luke 10:42 The story of Mary and Martha. Mary sat at Jesus' feet, listening to his words. Martha was busy preparing the meal. Both loved Jesus while serving him in different ways. However, Jesus said that Mary had chosen better. The implication is that before serving others, we need to spend time with Jesus. Pray in your own words. It is not necessary to use stilted or liturgical language. Talk as though God is your friend and collaborator.

PRAYER BEADS

Pearls of Prayer

I would like to share with you an alternative style of praying using Prayer Beads called, *Pearls of Prayer*. The *Pearls of Prayer* was conceived by Lutheran Bishop Lennobo of Sweden. Rev. Stephen Winemiller of Faith Lutheran Church in Sarasota, Florida adapted the beads as I use them and is the format included in this book. I have also included the directions for making your own beads of prayer. If you can string a bead on a string or elastic cord and tie a knot you can make prayer beads.

The purpose of the beads is to simplify and enhance your prayer life They give some structure while being totally flexible to your prayer moment. You can take as little or as long a time as you wish. You can pray on each bead or skip some. The moment is yours to chat with God. I did not make mine exactly as the directions specify. Rather, I tailored mine to what is meaningful to me. I've made many *Pearls of Prayer* and no two are alike. For example, I used a large yellow bead for God. Yellow is the color of sunshine. Have you heard the song, *You Are My Sunshine*? I've sung it to my grandchildren and sometimes sing it to God. He is my sunshine. Instead of a totally black bead to symbolizes sin and death, I use a black bead with some white in it. We all have our dark moments and places but we can overcome them with the help of God. Dying can be a painfully dark experience. Death, however, is a transition to a brighter more peaceful way of living. It is not the end. Grieve not the departed. Grieve the living left behind. The last bead symbolizes forgiveness and resurrection. A cross or butterfly shaped bead or charm is very appropriate there. A simplified Pearls of Prayer can be modified for children using fewer beads. For men, I use mostly wooden beads. You can also use beads to symbolize something specific such as family, peace, healing, forgiveness, relationships, society, children or whatever is important to you. I often light candles when using the prayer beads and especially like sitting outside in nature while praying with the beads. The silence beads are important because they help you to take a few moments to quiet your mind and let God speak to you.

*Supplies for making the *Pearls of Prayer can be found at most craft stores like Michaels and Joanne Fabrics which are often on sale. There are also numerous online sites.*

Prayer Beads Instructions

The length of cord used will depend on the size of the beads chosen for making your prayer beads. Whether using elastic or plain cording add length for tying a square knot. Some people prefer elastic because they wear the beads as a bracelet. Attaching a hair or paper clip to one end of the cord while stringing the beads will prevent the beads from slipping off the cord. A cloth at your work space helps keep beads from rolling off the table. Below is a GUIDE of the order of stringing the beads and their symbolism. The important thing is that the prayer beads will be meaningful to you. You can also make a prayer circle with beads to represent different issues you pray for such as a beads for peace, family, healing, thanks, purpose etc.. Gathering with friends to make the prayer bead circles is a great option. According to the guide below, begin with the God bead.

God bead - Large bead = God is the beginning and has no end. God is everywhere.
Me bead - Smaller bead = We are small compared to God. God made us and loves us.
Baptism bead - white/blue = God's commitment to His children and our commitment to God
Silence bead - small bead = Prayer is a conversation. Allow God to speak to you.
Creation bead - Green = God's amazingly beautiful creation. Circle of seasons and life

Silence bead
Desert bead - Brown = The hard times, challenges, feeling dried up. Suffering
Ocean bead - Blue = The good times. Always something to be thankful for.
Silence bead
People you love - Red or heart = Thanks for the people that add meaning in our lives.
People who love you - Red or heart = Thanks for mentors, parents, children, ancestors etc.
Not so lovable people - Smaller Red = We need to pray for them too.
Silence bead
The Word - beige = Spiritual power in the word that teaches and nourishes our soul
Silence bead
Sacrament bead - Purple = Wine in Holy Communion- A new promise of life forever
Silence bead
The Trinity beads - 3 gold = God is Father, Son and Holy Spirit
Silence bead
Sin/Death - Black with white = Admit hang-ups and dark places. Death is scary, however the white symbolizes that there is always hope in any circumstance and sin is forgiven.
Silence bead
Resurrection/Forgiveness - White, silver or a cross/butterfly = Forgiveness and life everlasting
Now knot the cord.

Pocket Prayer Cloth

The easy to make prayer cloths can be given to children to put under their pillow or to hold when they say their good night prayers. They can be gifted when someone is visiting shut-ins, cancer patients or someone in the hospital. They can be sent to someone in the military to be placed in their helmets. The pocket prayers are given to veterans in military hospitals by several churches. The Prayer Clothes are a reminder that God is near and God cares for the recipient of the Prayer Cloth. Making the Pocket Prayer Cloths can be a thoughtful ministry for an individual or church group. Batches of them could also be blessed by your priest or pastor before gifting them.

Instructions:

Need: 2 small pieces of cloth the same size -1 cross cut from contrasting fabric–pinking shears (optional)

Sew a simple fabric cross either by hand or machine onto a small piece of fabric. The sizes can vary. 3 X 5 or 31/2 by 51/2 is a nice size. Then a matching piece of fabric is sewn with a zigzag stitch for the back of the cloth. The edges are cut with a pinking shears. A card can be tied to or included in a zip lock bag with the Prayer Cloth.

Front of Card: He who dwells in the shelter of the Most High who abides in the shadow of the Almighty, will say to the Lord, "My Refuge and my fortress; my God, in whom I trust". Psalm 91:1-2 RSV May the love of God and His peace surround, strengthen and comfort you.

Back of Card: Pocket prayer clothes are small to fit into a pocket or helmet, held in the hand or put under a pillow. They are a visible and touchable reminder that you are honored and held in prayer. (Optional addition) Made by... the group or church name of who made the prayer cloth

SOME THOUGHTS TO PONDER

I am Thankful

- I am thankful for the enriching history of my ancestors who lived their faith in their hearts and passed on their values through the generations.
- I am thankful for indoor plumbing
- I am thankful for beautiful butterflies and hummingbirds that grace my garden in the summer.
- I am thankful for computers even though they are both a curse and a blessing.
- I am thankful for pets that bless our lives in many ways.
- I am glad I don't have to eat manna 7 days a week. Or any food 7 days a week for over a month.
- I am grateful for the prayers and support of my family and friends during challenging times.
- I am thankful for heat during the cold days of Winter.
- I am thankful that spiders don't fly.
- I am thankful for chocolate chip cookies
- I am thankful for caring doctors and nurses
- I am thankful for Oprah and the positive messages she spreads.
- I am thankful for seekers of truth
- I'm glad my mom didn't sew my mouth shut when I was a teen
- I am thankful for the miracle of birth
- I am thankful for the awesome beauty of nature created by God
- I am thankful for flush toilets
- I am thankful for safe drinking water
- I am thankful for all the veterans who sacrificed their limbs, minds and lives for freedom
- I am thankful for laughter
- I am thankful God loves me
- I am thankful for...................

Thoughts to Selah

Selah means to pause and think for a moment or moments to ponder. Below are some thoughts you may want to think about and expand on. You could pick one to think about for a day.

- Is there a difference between being religious and being spiritual? Am I religious, spiritual or both?
- Is my purpose in life connecting with my creator?
- When I transition from this life to the next I will have energy, purpose and fun.
- Jesus loves me
- What will be my legacy?
- The best and most beautiful things in life are free
- When God calls, how will I answer?
- "Knock Knock" " Who's there?" Revelations 3:20 How will I answer when God knocks?
- Since we are created in God's image and humanity has a sense of humor, then God smiles and laughs.
- What does Jesus think of me? If I could see myself as God sees me, I would not be insecure. I would be confident.
- *The two most important days in your life are the day you were born and the day you figure out why.* Mark Twain
- AMEN is an ! not a .[period] (Amen means, I agree or so be it.) It is called to be a verb and we are called to action. Therefore the prayers are not ended when we say, Amen.
- Do angels fart? A four year old boy, who will not be named, asked this question.
- When someone meditates, God teaches
- Wise men are still seeking Jesus
- I want to feel OK serving outside of my comfort zone
- When I am lonely or bored, get to know God.
- A grain of wheat remains a solitary grain until it falls into the ground and dies; but if it dies, it bears a rich harvest. (John 12:24 NEB). What in me needs to die before I can know God more intimately and serve God more enthusiastically?
- What are the sparks that light my fires of enthusiasm and curiosity?

God is More Than

God is a real being- an entity, yet much more than that
God is love and much more-
God is within me and all humanity and so much more-
God is creator of all things- and more-
God is energy and so much more-
God is a spiritual being and so much more-
God is my Savior and more-
God is...................... and much more

CPSIA information can be obtained at www.ICGtesting.com
Printed in the USA
BVOW03s2028170315

392137BV00001B/1/P